The Relationship
between C. G. Jung and
Erich Neumann Based
on Their Correspondence

The Relationship between C. G. Jung and Erich Neumann Based on Their Correspondence

MICHA NEUMANN

CHIRON PUBLICATIONS
ASHEVILLE, NORTH CAROLINA

Book and cover design by Marianne Jankowski.
Printed in the United States of America.

Library of Congress Cataloging-in-Publication Data
Names: Neumann, Micha, author.
Title: The relationship between C. G. Jung and Erich Neumann based on
  their correspondence / Micha Neumann.
Description: Asheville, North Carolina : Chiron Publications, [2015] |
  Includes bibliographical references and index.
Identifiers: LCCN 2015048618| ISBN 9781630512194 (pbk. : alk. paper) |
  ISBN 9781630512200 (hardcover : alk. paper)
Subjects: LCSH: Jung, C. G. (Carl Gustav), 1875-1961--Friends and
  associates--Correspondence. | Neumann, Erich--Friends and
  associates--Correspondence. | Psychoanalysts--Correspondence. |
  Psychoanalysts--Biography.
Classification: LCC BF109.J8 N48 2015 | DDC 150.19/540922--dc23
LC record available at http://lccn.loc.gov/2015048618

Contents

Acknowledgments

At the end of 1959 I finished medical school in Jerusalem and at the beginning of 1960 I started my psychiatric training. I wanted to have a personal training analysis and consulted my father about it. He recommended I start with a psychoanalytical Freudian analysis, because the very few Jungian analysts that my father mentioned were people I knew personally.

Following my father's advice I started psychoanalysis and my training at the psychoanalytic institute in Jerusalem. I am very grateful to him that, in line with his broad and creative spirit, he thought about what would be best for me and did not demand adherence and loyalty to his way. He thought that I should undergo analysis, and since it was impossible for me to go to a Jungian analyst, he encouraged me to go into Freudian analysis. He said that for the problems of my young age, Freudian analysis can be okay and even fruitful for me, and so it was.

Less than a year after the beginning of my residency training and personal analysis, my father died on November 5, 1960. There was only a short time to discuss with him my impressions of the first psychiatric patients with whom I worked and the professional literature that I had started to study. I knew from my father that his teacher, whom he loved and admired, was C. G. Jung, whose photo was always on my father's desk.

Only after my mother's death, in 1985, did I see for the first time the correspondence between Erich Neumann and Jung. A whole new world was opened to me, and I was amazed and most enthusiastic about these two outstanding personalities and their close ties and mutual admiration.

Reading their letters I felt that Jung was a positive and supportive father figure for my father, and I recalled that the relationship between Jung and his mentor and father figure, Sigmund Freud, was negative, not supportive in any way and even resentful.

I wrote this book in the early 1990s after I had published several articles on this topic in Hebrew, German, and English, but I knew that it could not be published before the publication of the complete Jung-Neumann correspondence. I had to wait many long years, working through the difficulties encountered in publishing the correspondence.

This book, in which I look into the relationship between C. G. Jung and Erich Neumann based on their correspondence, is both personal and professional. It is with satisfaction that I conclude that in spite of their differences and arguments, the relationship between Jung and Neumann remained open and creative till the end of their lives.

I am grateful to Dr. Nancy Swift Furlotti, who made the publication of this book, as well as the publication of *Analytical Psychology in Exile*, possible through a donation from the Furlotti Family Foundation.

It is with the continuous and relentless efforts and perseverance of Dr. Erel Shalit that this undertaking has been brought to its fruitful conclusion.

I owe a special thanks to the Foundation for the Works of C. G. Jung for granting permission to quote from the letters of C. G. Jung and to Andreas Jung for his interest and support.

I wish to thank Ruth Ammann and the C. G. Jung Institute, Zurich, for granting permission to use the photo of C. G. Jung.

Also, I want to express my gratitude to Drs. Steven Buser and Len Cruz of Chiron Publications, who have seen the value of this book, as well as Siobhan Drummond, who has done an excellent job as editor, and Marianne Jankowski for the design of the book and the cover.

Parts of this book have appeared in the following journals, all having granted permission to include material here, for which I thank them:

The German language *Jungian Analytical Psychological Journal*; *Harvest*; *Sichot—Dialog, Israel Journal of Psychotherapy*; *Ostterreichische Gesellschaft fur Analytische Psychologie*.

Last but not least, I want to thank Martin Liebscher, who edited *Analytical Psychology in Exile: The Correspondence of C. G. Jung and Erich Neumann*, and Fred Appel and Princeton University Press for permission to quote from the letters. Thanks also to Heather McCartney, the translator of both *Analytical Psychology in Exile* and this book.

Professor M. Neumann

Introduction

The encounter between Erich Neumann and Carl Gustav Jung is intrinsically interesting, indeed, all the more so when their relationship is compared with the more complicated relationship between Jung and Sigmund Freud. The relationship between Jung and Neumann was at first one of teacher and pupil. When they met for the first time, Neumann was twenty-eight years old and Jung fifty-nine. Neumann was a young doctor, a Jew and a Zionist, who left Germany immediately after Hitler seized power.

At that time, Jung had an internationally respected position as a psychiatrist, psychologist, and therapist. Moreover, he was also the founder and leader of the field of international scientific analytical psychology and its organization. The years of the stormy battles with Freud were, at that time, already twenty years in the past.[1]

In the Freud-Jung relationship, Freud was the elder, the man with standing and position, and Jung was the young pupil who had to fight for his ideas and his autonomy. This complicated relationship reached its ultimate breakdown in 1913, after Jung had withdrawn from the International Society of Psychoanalysis and from the editorial board of the *Psychoanalytic Journal*. The central theme of their quarrel was Jung's distancing himself from and critique of important components of Freudian psychoanalytic theory.

Freud defended his theoretical system very forcefully and was intolerant of Jung's ideas. He did not make any serious efforts to understand them and to incorporate them into his theoretical framework. He regarded Jung's ideas as dangerous for the integrity of his theoretical structure. Jung felt that Freud demanded loyalty from him even at the cost of his scientific and creative freedom, and this he refused to surrender.

Freud unconsciously behaved toward Jung as though to a beloved son and successor ("my crown prince") and, conversely, as though to a treacherous son who murders his father and seeks to destroy his reputation.

Jung regarded Freud as a great man, a teacher and father, but as a despotic and repressive father who does not recognize the maturity and autonomy of his son. He was very wounded by this relationship, experienced it as contemptuous, callous, and arrogant, and he separated from Freud in a painful crisis.

It is important to determine here that it was not only differences of professional opinion which played a role in this affair. The break between Jung and Freud also had other causes which arose out of cultural and national backgrounds. On the one hand, Freud was an assimilated European Jew, who had grown up in Vienna and who identified with the scientific, medical, and neurological viewpoints and conceptions of his time, whereas Jung was situated as his polar opposite: a Swiss Protestant, the son of a pastor, who, although a doctor, was attracted to occult phenomena and was interested in philosophy, mythology, psychology, and mysticism.

Psychoanalysis achieved particular support and special interest among the Jews who belonged to Freud's social and cultural circle, and most of his pupils, followers, and colleagues belonged to the same national-religious group, whereas Jung's Swiss group came from a variety of quite different backgrounds. Soon the differences between Vienna and Zurich assumed the character of the differences between Jews and Christians hostile to one another. Jung suffered from this undisguised animosity and linked this way of relating to him to the fact that he was not a Jew. He had to endure their unrelenting accusations that he was anti-Semitic.

Under these historical circumstances and, given the emotional wounds in Jung's psyche, it is particularly interesting to elucidate how the relationship developed between him and his Jewish pupil, Erich Neumann. Did Jung support his creative and original colleague, whose ideas were not accepted in the Jungian circles in Zurich? Are there parallels or similarities between the Freud-Jung relationship and the Jung-Neumann relationship? Did Jung behave differently in his role as a father figure toward Neumann from how he had been treated in his role of a son by Freud? How did the relationship between Jew-

ish Zionist Neumann and his Christian Swiss teacher, thirty years his
senior, develop?

What follows is an account of the relationship between the two.
The original manuscript, written nearly thirty years ago, was based on
Jung's letters to various people, which have been published in three
volumes and include twenty letters to Neumann, written between
1934 and 1959, and three letters from Jung to Neumann written in
1934 and 1935. Since then, the correspondence between Jung and
Neumann has been published, and the letters excerpted here are taken
from that new collection.[2]

Another source for the depiction of this relationship are the author's impressions gleaned from his parents regarding Jung, who was
always a central and positive presence in the home of Erich and Julie
Neumann.

Erich Neumann in Berlin

Erich Neumann was born in 1905 in Berlin as the youngest son of Eduard and Selma Neumann. His father was a prosperous businessman who considered himself a German citizen of the Mosaic religion. From his youth Neumann was engaged with cultural and intellectual problems. He was especially interested in literature and philosophy, as well as history and the destiny of the Jewish people. His older brother enlisted in the German army and fought in the First World War.

This was the first war in which Jews participated in the various national armies of Europe and the United States, fighting on both sides. They did this in full identification with the national ideals and objectives of the states in which they lived. It was a tragic situation that led to Jews fighting against each other for the first time, out of loyalty to their respective homelands, which had afforded them emancipation and civil equality.

This tragic Jewish reality made a great impression on Neumann. He grew up in post-war Berlin, in the democratic atmosphere of the Weimar Republic. In these years there was a particular cultural expansion and revival throughout Germany, especially in Berlin. Berlin was a lively cultural capital in which art, music, literature, and the sciences flourished. The German Jews played a significant role in this cultural revival, and their participation was also important in economic and political life. The success of the Jews and the fact that they commanded many important positions aroused and fostered envy and anti-Semitism, which was exploited by Hitler and the growing National Socialist German Workers' Party to strengthen their hold on power.

Erich Neumann graduated from high school and studied philosophy at Berlin University. His doctoral dissertation in 1926 was on the

German philosopher and philologist Johann Arnold Kanne. Following this, he studied medicine with the intention of pursuing psychiatry and psychotherapy, an aim that was also the impetus for his medical studies.

During all these years he continued with the study of Judaism, Hasidism, and Kabbalah (Jewish mysticism), as well as that of psychology. He read Freud's works with great interest but was particularly keen on Jung's writings. He admired Jung's great knowledge of culture and art, of mythology and the roots of Western civilization. The exploration of his Jewish roots occupied Neumann very much, and through this, as well as through the influence of his Zionist wife, he became convinced that the return of the Jews to Palestine was a real, personal, and intellectual necessity, based on actual personal and collective psychological reality.

The First Encounter with Jung

In 1933, after he had completed his medical studies and when Hitler came to power, Neumann left Germany and set off for Palestine. On his way, he stayed several months in Zurich, where he had his first, very productive encounter with Jung, with whom he was in analysis. Neumann developed strong feelings of respect, admiration, and gratitude toward Jung, and Jung gave his young colleague and student much support, encouragement, and esteem. In the years 1933–1934, firm foundations were laid for their enduring collaboration and friendship.

Jung's Relationship with the Jews and Allegations of Anti-Semitism

During Neumann's work with Jung, they often conversed a great deal about Jews and Judaism. They naturally also discussed the phenomenon of National Socialism. Neumann, who had experienced the vicious anti-Semitism of the Nazis in Germany firsthand, attempted to persuade Jung of the terrible dangers of the National Socialist movement and its brutal inhumanity. He advised Jung to speak out frankly and clearly against their ideologies, particularly against their toxic anti-Semitism. He admitted to me that he had not been able to alter Jung's position and stance. Neumann regarded Jung's stance on National Socialism as completely wrong, as a serious error, as a personal weakness and a blind spot, but he did not permit this shadow side of Jung to overshadow their special, remarkable relationship. Despite Neumann's critique of Jung's attitude in these years, their friendship survived this argument.

Jung, who believed in the qualities of the collective German unconscious, insisted on his opinion that something positive would still emerge from the situation.[3] My father warned Jung that if he continued to be silent about the Jews at such an evil time, it would always be remembered and he would never be forgiven. In summary, I must observe that a stack of written evidence exists which substantiates the allegations of Jung's anti-Semitism.

Jung's article "The State of Psychotherapy Today," which was published in March 1934, was criticized as being Nazi-friendly and anti-Semitic, and Neumann was understandably furious about it.[4] In response to the article, he wrote his first letter to Jung while still in Switzerland and still an analysand and student of Jung. The letter, which is undated, reads:

When I spoke—in some dismay—with Miss Wolff today about the partial validity of Dr. Bally's article and she gave me your paper "The State of Psychotherapy Today," I could not have imagined what a controversy of such fateful personal significance was about to unfold! I know I don't have to tell you what you mean to me, and how hard it is for me to disagree with you, but I feel I simply must take issue with you on a matter that goes far beyond any merely personal concerns. I will refrain from commenting on whether the reverberations that your words are bound to have were indeed what you intended, and I will be silent about whether it is truly a Goethe-inspired perspective to view the emergence of National Socialism in all its human-lashing, bloodthirsty barbarianism as a "mighty presence" in the Germanic unconscious. I will also ignore the fact that I am perplexed that—though you cited in your lecture "the more obscure reference" to the ecstatic "Allah il Allah" wail and that you spoke out against the idea of the "Führer as idol"— here you are asserting that "a movement that takes hold of an entire nation, already has each and every individual in its grip." As a Jew, I do not feel I have any license to intervene in a controversy that no German can avoid today when they encounter this Germanic unconscious, but as it is certainly correct that we Jews are accustomed to recognizing the shadow-side, then I cannot comprehend why a person like you cannot see what is all too cruelly obvious to everyone these days—that it is also in the Germanic psyche (and in the Slavic one) that a mind-numbing cloud of filth, blood and rottenness is brewing.

It may well be that the immemorial history of my people with its long recurrence of prophets, judges, Zaddikim and elders fills me with implausible and completely un-Germanic ideas (un-Germanic for sure), but, where I come from, great men have always been called upon to exercise discernment and to stand against the crowd—and it is precisely my conviction about the uniqueness of your own nature which causes me now—(not only in my own interest)—to ask you if this easy affirmation, this throwing yourself into the frenzy of Germanic exuberance—is this your true position or do I misunderstand you on this point?

More importantly though, I would wish to disabuse you of the conviction that Jews are as you imagine them to be. I do not know the Jews you have treated, but I know you consider even my friend Gerhard Adler to be exceptionally Jewish. I believe myself to be completely certain of his agreement when I say to you that, even among our own people, things are not so unfortunate as for either of us to be considered typical representatives.

The rather sad Jewish remnants which have wound their way to you are those that remain, the most diasporic, assimilated and nationalized Jews, individuals and stragglers, but from where, dear Dr. Jung, do you know the Jewish race, the Jewish people? May your error of judgment perhaps be conditioned (in part) by the general ignorance of things Jewish and the secret and medieval abhorrence of them that thus leads to knowing everything about the India of 2,000 years ago and nothing about the Hasidism of 150 years ago? Furthermore, is there not the remnant of a misunderstanding in a sentence such as: "The Aryan unconscious has a higher potential than the Jewish (one)" which allows a primitive race to claim that "they are the ones who are." The Hasidism movement as well as that of Zionism demonstrate the inexhaustible liveliness of the Jewish people, as only a deficient interest can overlook the outrageousness of a phenomenon such as, for example, the renaissance of the Hebrew language that was dead for 2,000 years and the settlement in Palestine that you, albeit tentatively and skeptically, consider to be romantic, while, as a Germanic person, you seem to wish to have a monopoly on all romanticism and illusion and value them highly. Of course I have to laugh at this exaggerated formulation, but there is much truth in what I am saying. This Jewish renaissance seems to me to be more embryonic, youthful and full of energy than the Nazi-rigid, brutally organized and stolid, extreme submissiveness of the Aryan revivals. Believe me, as a Jew, I quite love the Germanic potential as far as I am able to see it and get a sense of it, but to equate National Socialism with the Aryan-Germanic is perhaps ominously incorrect and I cannot understand how you reach this conclusion and whether you must reach it. Is Bolshevism also a feature of the Aryan unconscious? Or what does it imply that there, as you told me, all bad instincts have been called upon—which is apparently completely different in Germany.

I believe, even, that in both there are seeds of things to come, but I believe and know I have learned from you, and had it confirmed by you, that the most precious secret of every human being—not only of the Germanic race—is, in essence, the purely creative prescient depths of one's soul. Far beyond the fact that your Jewish diagnosis is not right, I simply cannot see that it is possible that the collective unconscious, in its deeper layers, can have greater or fewer tensions within it among the different races. It seems to me that, as is the case for the individual, it is contingent on the consciousness of the race that changes through history and that, expressly in the case of the Jewish people, has changed repeatedly and will change again, and this engenders new developments over and over again. I fear you are confusing Freud—whom you have classified sociologically as European by the way—with the Jew, and therefore the use of Nazi terminology—simply to identify Freud's categories as "Jewish categories"—is doubly puzzling coming from your pen, especially when previously—before the rise of Hitler—Freud's extraverted theory was contrasted with Adler's introverted theory.

I do not wish to change anything in this letter. It will remain as it is written. Hopefully you will appreciate how it is intended. It seems to me that it is precisely my gratitude toward you that obliges me to be candid. I hope there is not too much "Mars" in this, but that there is some "Mars" here, I know, and I stand by it. [APE, 4N, pp. 10–15]

Neumann is furious and hurt by Jung's formulations, yet describes them as "misunderstandings."

Neumann in Palestine

Erich Neumann arrived in Palestine in the summer of 1934. It is interesting to read the young German-Jewish intellectual's impressions of and reactions to his encounter with the Palestine of that time and the collision between dream and reality.

The encounter with the non-pioneer element of the East European Jewish lower middle classes in Tel Aviv was a type of culture shock for Neumann.

In the summer of 1934 Neumann wrote another undated letter to Jung:

> I did not, by any means, come here with any illusions, but what I have found extraordinary was that I haven't found a "people" here with whom I fundamentally feel I belong. I might have known that before, of course, but it was not the case, and the fact that the Jews here as a people, as a not-yet-people, seemed so extremely needy was a shock at first. On the other hand, though, the landscape gripped me in such a compelling way that I couldn't ever have thought possible. Precisely from the place I hadn't expected it, a vantage point emerged. I haven't fully made sense of this. Anyhow, as you prophesied, the anima has gone to ground. . . .
>
> The situation here is exceedingly serious, as I see it. The original spiritual, idealistic forces who established the country, the core of the working class and of the land settlements are being repressed by a growing wave of undifferentiated, egotistic, short-sighted, entrepreneurial Jews, flooding here because of the economic opportunities. Thanks to this, everything is escalating more and more, and a growing politicization of the best is obstructing all horizons. But

this politicization is inevitable as the situation of the country is devoid of all state authority and gives power to the negative individual like nowhere else does. So everything points to fascism regardless of where it might originate. As a people, the Jews are infinitely more stupid than I expected, . . . [APE, 5N, pp. 16–17]

Here we can see that even in 1934, before the Holocaust and before mass emigration of the Jews to Israel, when the older Jewish community (the so-called Yishuv) was still very small, Neumann saw with shocking clarity the problems and dangers that still occupy us today, more than eighty years later. Neumann continues his letter:

Please don't misunderstand me—I am not reproaching the Jew. How could it be any different? We come, as individuals, from who knows where and are then supposed to be one people. That all takes time, but I must state it as it is. So, I believe, the situation is rather muddled—but I'm not qualified politically and I haven't been here long—and herein lies my hope. I can well imagine that Palestine will get dangerously close to the abyss and I assume that the Jews, in a paradoxical situation, will then come to their senses—as ever. Everywhere the economy is booming, it's all hard work and speculation. There is little interest in intellectual things except among the workers and almost none in things Jewish. A newly prospering petit bourgeois middle class is evident everywhere, not only in Tel Aviv. [APE, 5N, p. 17]

Unsettled by the force of his criticism, he sought to temper it. He explains:

All of this is quite natural. We find ourselves in a strongly extraverted phase—how else could Palestine be developed? The Jews are coming to a—terrible—civilization. It cannot be changed. [APE, 5N, p. 17]

Neumann is very affected by the tremendous differences. He considers the East European orthodoxy as being very alien to him and his central European values:

The traditionlessness of this struggle that has no core gives everything a rather ghostly demeanor. It is a people of infinite opposites.
What orthodoxy does exist here is so immeasurably foreign to me
that I'm shaken by it. Alongside this are the unprincipled specula-
tors and then the hordes of people who, by the investment of their
substance, have constructed the prettiest villages and landscapes out
of deserts and swamps. . . . [APE, 5N, pp. 17–18]

Neumann quickly realized after he had arrived in Palestine that
there was no prospect of his taking root in the new country. It would
only be possible for the second generation of European settlers to really put down roots and to feel themselves to be full and true children
of the new homeland. He knows that he and his generation belong
to the interim generation, the "desert generation." He continues his
letter to Jung:

It is strange to recognize that my generation will only be an interim
generation here—our children will be the first ones to form the
basis of a nation. We are Germans, Russians, Poles, Americans etc.
What an opportunity it will be when all the cultural wealth that we
bring with us is really assimilated into Judaism. I don't share your
opinion at all that there will be no Alexandrianism here, but rather,
either nothing at all or something completely new, if, as I believe,
despite everything, the Jews have retained their incredible ability to
assimilate.

The way forward, as I see it, is certainly as hard as it is dangerous. I actually fear that all our repressed instincts, all our desires
for power and revenge, all our mindlessness and hidden brutality
will be realized here. Indeed, the ongoing development of the Jews
failed precisely because, on the one hand, they were united in a
collective-religious bond and, on the other, they were under pressure from other nations as individuals. After the emancipation they
caught up unnaturally quickly and powerfully with the Western
trend toward the individual (secularization, rationalization, extra-
version, the break with the continuity of the past), and thereby the
shadow was finally "liberated," and here in Palestine it can reveal
itself for the first time as, here, there is no external pressure. That
will not be pleasant— [APE, 5N, p. 18]

After the great hope, a great fear arises. In an almost prophetic sense, he had foreseen the great dangers of the impending shadow when the Jewish community in Palestine was still very sparse and small (450,000 Jews), less than a third of the Arab population. Neumann grapples with this, and it is clear that he oscillates between hope and concern:

> Perhaps we will all be killed, but it's no use—it simply must be out in the open at last and worked through. (I wonder often if I am projecting all of this, but it does seem to me to be more than mere projection.) In the face of this apparently historic necessity, the chaos here becomes not only bearable to me but I also feel myself to be infinitely closely bound up with it; I emerge out of this to my own "people." I must, though, confess that I am quite often afraid at the same time. I feel myself here to be quite accountable and I still know that my place is here, quite independently from whether the Jews will grant me this place one day or not. . . . [APE, 5N, p. 18–19]

He writes further:

> I'd like to add something else too. I've set myself the big challenge of getting you to write something fundamental about Judaism. I believe I can only do this by simply speaking to you about what is very important to me. [APE, 5N, p. 20]

At the end of his letter, he writes:

> I have considered myself (and still do) to be very attached to you and your work—does this oblige me to a public conformity with your students? I would be very concerned if that were the case, but I am convinced that it is not so. . . . [APE, 5N, p. 21]

And then:

> Dear Dr. Jung, it still seems too crass simply to thank you for what I have received from you; I am ambitious enough to say that I hope to be able to give something to you in return too. I don't think it is that I cannot say thank you—that is just not enough. [APE, 5N, pp. 21–22]

This letter, written at the age of only twenty-eight, is very impressive in the depth of his sensitivity and in the austerity of his perceptions. He grasps the problems of how a new, unified, and cultivated nation can be created in the land of Israel (Eretz Israel). His vision is grounded in strong feelings of confidence and hope. The unapologetic openness expressed in this letter indicates the deep and close relationship between Neumann and Jung, and at the end of the letter a strong attachment and a deep gratitude is conveyed.

While Neumann was still living in Zurich and working with Jung, they decided that they would discuss the Jewish problem and questions of Judaism and Zionism in their planned correspondence. Neumann asked Jung to comment on this subject matter. He hoped Jung would devote himself to this problem with the same eagerness that he invested in the myths of the Christian Middle Ages and the remote cultures of the East.

Although Jung apparently did not reply to all of Neumann's letters, Neumann does not let up. On 19 July 1934 Neumann writes to Jung:

> I have firmly resolved not to let up, so I must warn you against me once again in good time. I have the firm intention not to give you any peace about the Jewish problem and, if necessary, I will earn again the lost tenacity and stubbornness of my race in order to be taken into the depths of these problems by you so that I no longer see them from a blinkered standpoint. I think I must also make a confession although it is not pleasant to do so. Before I came to you, I was rather sad that I was not able to go to a Jewish authority because I wanted to go to a "teacher" and I found it typified precisely the decline of Judaism that it had no such authoritative personality in its ranks. With you, I became aware of what was prototypical in my situation. According to Jewish tradition, there are Zaddikim of the nations, and that is why the Jews have to go to the Zaddikim of the nations—perhaps that is why they do not have any of their own left. This Jewish situation, the beginning of an exchange, of an understanding *sub specie dei*—this is what makes this "letter exchange" so important to me. [APE, 6N, pp. 35–36]

In the next letters, Jung made a certain effort to state his position on the questions that so engaged Neumann, but outside of this correspondence Jung could not be prevailed upon to immerse himself further in Judaism and Jewish mysticism. Jung applied his psychological concepts to understanding historical and cultural processes, but for reasons which are not clear, he did not take up the challenge of the study and a deeper understanding of Jewish culture that was so important for Neumann.

Jung wrote Neumann a letter on 12 August 1934:

> I do not believe that the Jews suffered from a collective neurosis until their emancipation. However, whether the emancipation itself did not have a neurotic effect seems questionable to me, and the matter requires some serious consideration. The social cohesiveness of the entire Jewish people was a parallel phenomenon to that of the spiritual and political situation of the Christian Middle Ages. With the emancipation of Christians from the authority of the Catholic church, unconscious archetypes were activated in the Christian unconscious that we are still processing—it is a type of digestive process that still continues and that has given rise to so-called neopagan developments in Germany that have obvious roots in the distant past and that are concessions to the power of pagan archetypes. I believe, therefore, that the emancipated Jew is equally threatened by an activation of the collective unconscious. For sure, one archetype is linked to the soil, and from this emerges the psychic necessity of Zionism; another archetype, having a compensatory relationship with rationalism, is connected with religious archetypes, hence the renewal of Hasidism in its more liberal cosmopolitan form, pretty much represented by Martin Buber. Insofar as these activated archetypes are not consciously assimilated, a neurotic condition can easily arise. In the Christian West, neurotic unrest is evident. . . .
>
> I know that the Jewish problem is, for you, a matter of the utmost seriousness—just as, for me, our spiritual condition and the psychic life of the individual's soul is the most important thing. You can therefore be sure that I will give my attention to this problematic issue using all available means, as it is for me of the utmost value to discuss the complex intricacies of modern culture and its psychic situation with a Jew who is expressly familiar with the European context and who is coming at this issue from

a slightly different perspective, while residing on his own archetypal soil.

. . . I was extremely interested to hear about your dreams and
of the transformations of the anima. A psychic blood transfusion!
[APE, 7J, pp. 51–54]

Now follow some quite astonishing lines in which Jung writes:

In reality, it seems to me, Jacob is the *quintessence* of the Jew and
therefore a symbolic attempt at a collective individuation, or
rather at individuation on a collective level. (Like, for example,
historically, Hitler represents the same for the Germans, or myth-
ically, we have Jesus, Mithras, Attis, Osiris, etc.) So you are quite
right in conceiving of the problem completely from the side of the
collective unconscious and in understanding Jacob entirely as a
symbolic exponent of folk psychology. This way of thinking takes
you furthest.

. . . .

The non-Jews as "world population" cannot fall into an "external" because they are already in it. They inhabit the centers
of mass population in the fertile regions. Their number and their
possession of the land are a counterweight to the "internal danger." Through his mere existence, the Jew draws attention to
these inconveniences. So he falls into the shadow realm of the
mass populations. These latter need no self-defense (except in
emergencies) and little intuition; rather, they need more sensation and aesthetic feeling (to be able to take advantage of a secure
life). In this way, they fall into the shadow of the Jews and can be
sure of his secret contempt, for they live in immoral peace with
all that the Jew illicitly desires. This ancient tranquility has been
sensitively upset by Jewish Christianity that, as far as the fateful
development of consciousness is concerned, was plainly necessary.
Only with the liberalization—i.e., with the decline of Christianity—as a consequence of the enlightenment, did the Jew receive
the reciprocal gift of the Danaans: the emancipation, and with
it the enjoyment of the world that goes against tradition and is
alienating from God, and that is always the fruit of a secure life.
[APE, 7J, pp. 54, 57]

The letter ends with the sentence: "What is the meaning of 'Galut' psychology? A puzzle."

A letter from Neumann to Jung, undated (probably autumn 1934):

> My last letter left me with something of a nasty aftertaste, and I now believe I know why. I got far too caught up in "praise of the Jews" and did not take into account nearly enough the fact that, at the same time, the Jews are always the most disappointing people of world history. And indeed not only that—all too many are willing to pay for the attitude toward the future with an impoverishment of the present. There's a nice, relevant Hasidic story about this. "After a Sabbath meal at which many Jewish fathers were present, Yehudi speaks: 'Well, people, if any of you are asked what is your purpose on earth, each one of you answers, "to raise my son to learn and to serve God." And when the son has grown up, he forgets his father's purpose on earth, and strives for exactly the same thing himself. And if you ask him the point of all this strife, he will tell you: "I have to raise my son in the doctrine and for good works." And thus it is, you people, from generation to generation. But when, finally, will we get to see the rightful child?'"
>
> We are not only living off the interest of old capital but now that this has been largely devalued by the inflation of emancipation, we are inclined to live on credit, while hoping for an upturn or even invoking one. This won't do, of course.
>
> I do not mean to say that what I wrote to you is wrong—I see quite factually the Jews are in a quite peculiar situation that is calculated to force them to find new and groundbreaking solutions, but one should not be awarding them laurels in advance, while it is still so terribly questionable whether they will succeed or whether they won't just fail as they nearly always do. No real disappointment in the failure of the Jews could dissuade me from believing in them because, out of the making conscious of their failure, a step forward has always emerged, but I wouldn't want to be "a gushing enthusiast in Israel"—that is not my role but rather my danger. I just wanted to write this to you in haste—that I have understood this in something of a new way again. I believe my opposition to some of your objections or alleged underestimations led me to overcompensate rather. [APE, 9N, pp. 77–78]

Neumann, who sees soberly, realistically, and clearly the disappointing reality of the fulfillment of the Zionist dream and of Jewish destiny (Light Unto the Nations), expresses his faith in the ability of the Jewish people to experience crises and failures and to always come through them having gained something positive and new, which he describes as a further expansion.

On 9 February 1935, Neumann congratulates Jung on becoming a professor:

> Although I can imagine that the Professorship comes all rather late in the day and elicits only an ironic smile from you, I would still like to say something to you in this regard. Certainly, despite everything, this Professorship is a signal . . . [APE, 12N, p. 84]

He complains about Jung's lack of written replies and hopes Jung will still write a book on the Jewish question.

> I regret very much of course that our correspondence that was and is very important to me has not been added to by another letter from you, but I know the demands of work that you are under and am now beginning, though with a heavy heart, to come to terms with writing fewer questions and working on more answers. But what about your book on the Jewish question? Was that only accepted by you in the heat of the moment or even only as a therapeutic ruse? [APE, 12N, pp. 84–85]

An undated letter (apparently dated 23 April 1935) from the same year reads:[5]

> Firstly I thank you for your letter that tempered my feeling that "[i]n the wide field I am alone." Humanly that is in no way the case, and the practice is going very well too, as are the courses, etc.
> . . . .
> I hope my future work on Hasidism will develop this. (By the way, "the Jews, the most unknown people"; did I read correctly Zarath II, p. 45, "Talmud, the Jewish book of mysteries"? As ever, such a sentence would not have been possible in the Club about a Chinese,

Indian, or Persian content, to say nothing of Gnosis, but the Jews are positioned apparently too elementally in close proximity.)
. . . .

In my experience, which is negligible when compared with yours, the expansion of psychic capacity leads to a general perception of the world, and this exceeds all individually conditioned formulas. An extraverted Indian and an introverted Jew will hold more in common or even identically after the individuation process than typologically different unconscious individuals from one race. . . .

It is rather unfortunate that there is no scientific discussion for Jungian students. What there is too much of in the case of the Freudians—journals always repeating the same thing—in your case there is too little. The not insignificant number of your students ought to have something to say about analytical psychology, even about new things. Or—which I would sadly be able to understand—maybe you prefer not to have your own material associated and confused with that of others about whose form and quality you are more or less in doubt? [APE, 14N, pp. 91, 94, 96]

On 27 April 1935, Jung wrote a long letter in which he attempts to respond to Neumann's many questions:

First and foremost my full apologies for tardy replies and such like. I gathered your correspondence together in order to reply *in globo* and then of course I did not have the time to do it. Recently there has been too much going on as well. However you must not assume that you make too many demands on my time. Sooner or later the moment will come when I can reply. I have promised you that after all. . . .

Each fundamental change in the psychological situation disposes of one psychological system of adaptation and requires a new one. Without conscious regard to this, archetypes arise in the intermediate arena that, as a rule, remain unconscious. They do not remain without influence on the subsequent events. Thus Zionism contains not a little from Jewish history, the reestablishment of Israel as a nation, perhaps fantasies about national kingship, etc. The archetypes become visible only indirectly, such as in the belligerent affectations of the Jewish National Socialists or in the corresponding fantasies of individuals, or in the revival of Hebrew as an everyday language. Now, the archetypes can be a danger in that they bring about an archaization of social and political events, or in that they arouse rationalistic and utopian reaction phenomena that are precisely designed to suppress the effect of the archetypes. The archaization reveals itself in Europe in the form of dictatorships with lictor bundles, roman greetings on the one hand, swastikas, Führer, heroism, the German race, etc. . . .

Without doubt you are correct if you reject my judgment of the Jews as I am only basing this on the external aspect. Every judgment, if it is to hold, must be one sided at first in order to be moderated later by more general observation. Everything that you criticize is therefore correct and I would have to feel most deeply affected on account of my one-sidedness if I had not been constantly conscious of this. . . .

. . . But what Koigen writes about Semites seems to my mind to be characteristic . . .

Koigen's differentiations are, on the whole, correct. Internally determined, prophetic, spirit-filled yearning and externally determined need that arouses the desire to take hold of the world and re-shape it, is characteristic of Semitic religious feeling. Equally typical for the "Indo-Germanic" is the feeling that resides in the world and its fullness that intuits higher being in the symbolization of becoming and passing away. ("All that must disappear is but a parable.") However one wishes to formulate this contrast, the main thing is that it exists and it expresses a peculiarly different temperament.

. . . We should therefore expect, if everything does not deceive, such manifestations in the later course of the psychological history of humanity as, say, National Socialism which, with the abundance of power of the "Führer," the total power of the state, the almost religious veneration of the swastika symbol and certain anti-Christian tendencies, to say nothing of the enthusiastic mass movement, demonstrates all the characteristics of an intermediate stage in Christ's original *process of becoming human*. That Hitler has been celebrated more than once as a "savior," indeed that his picture occasionally even adorned an altar, and that the swastika has not stopped even in front of church doors, proves the expansion or the descent of the God-manhood into the regions of humanization or the rise of a new notion in the German, which he anyway experiences falsely—or psychologically correctly—in fatal dependence on Jewish priority (*hinc illae lacrimae*) as the chosenness of the blond and blue-eyed race. . . .

. . . The church is an ideal substitute for the chosenness of the people and because spiritual, therefore universal, in contrast to the racial ties of the Jews 'in the circumcision." Inasmuch as you regard individuation as a "universal" metaphysical task even for the Jews, you concur with my view, but you put yourself at odds with your historical determinedness. I do the same, however, but in line with my expositions above with less historical discrepancy, as I am "only" attached to the confession of an *idea*, but not historically to the "people within me." The "tribal" national bonds with their secluded character seem to me—quite separately from their historical-psychological significance—to be a primitive relic, in comparison to the constantly evolving development in the Christian world of ideas, which only gives the impression of being still identical with the worldviews of early Christianity and which, in any case, was never a national bond, but was, from the very beginning, principally universal.

Contemporary events in Germany are in a certain sense a countermovement to the world-weariness of the German, which he certainly used to be quite proud of—not quite without good reason—, and, at the same time, it is a return to this same primitive relic, the tribal bond, which wishes to draw religion once again into its circle of influence. But this is taking place back to front: the Jewish racial bond was a result of the covenant with God, whereas the political racial bond would even like to nationalize God. The spiritual secularization of the Germans stood in contradiction to its actual national and physical bonds; therefore, sooner or later something had to happen to show him what's what. The Heavenly Father has long since known this and this is why it is completely superfluous to annex him to the German nation. The wheels of history cannot be reversed. [APE, 15J, pp. 98–104, 106–107]

A letter from Neumann to Jung from 29 October 1935:

The work on the Jewish material that is slow and difficult. Gropingly I feel for contours, difficult because I am myself only gradu-

ally starting to grasp where analytical psychology cannot fully be
the ground on which I stand. That does not mean that I am not
standing on the ground of analytical psychology, more than ever
I believe I sense its central significance for me. What is self-evident is becoming clearer to me—that analytical psychology itself
has a foundation that is in part so self-evident that it can only become conscious of itself in part. Switzerland—Germany, the West,
Christianity. Not a discovery, and yet it is one after all. I must learn
to distinguish. It is difficult when so much weight lies on the other
side, it is certainly easier to do as "your Jews" do and to assimilate, such as Westmann, Kirsch, but this would only mean avoiding
one's own individuation that must be achieved, despite everything,
on the collective-archetypally different foundation. . . . Analytical
psychology, not yet fully realized, also holds this danger—that of
the betrayal of one's own foundation in favor of a "nicer," "more
advanced" and "more modern" one. . . . You have not worked
through the whole of Christianity in vain—I still think that Judaism is missing. . . .

The way in which your being Swiss, Christian, and a Western
man is self-evident differentiates you centrally, and not only you,
from the way in which it is not self-evident that Jews are Jews. Do
you, in fact, underestimate the significance of this point in the analysis of Jews? You did express to me once your abhorrence toward
this phenomenon of self-betrayal but I have not noticed anywhere
that you have tangibly nailed it down. Please do not misunderstand
this to be impudence; as a question it is important to me. . . . Even
you would like to "make use of" the ideology of the Jews being
leaven for the European culture. They are indeed quite serviceable
in this way, but there remain protected Jews in the psychological
sense, without foundation, i.e., without the possibility of individuation. The relationship of the Jews to the "earth" is, in a fundamental way, the same as for the Gentiles and Christians on a Gentile
basis, but this problem can be resolved neither by a simple return
to the soil (political Zionism) nor by only a psychical return to the
soil (the Galut Jew with analytical psychology). Both of these must
be achieved together. The environment of the Jew in Europe is
the collective unconscious of the non-Jews, and with this, his individuation is impossible. Only among Jews was it and is it possible,

for only there does he encounter his archetypal foundation in the world and only in collision with this, can he—at best—achieve individuation. All these problems keep me occupied and will not allow me respite from this incessant work. So, I am well. [APE, 17N, pp. 115–117]

Jung replies to Neumann's letter on 22 December 1935:

Do not allow yourself to go gray over missing my 60th birthday. The abstract number 60 means nothing at all to me. I much prefer to know, through hearing from you, what you are doing. What the European Jews are doing I already know, but what the Jews are doing on archetypal soil—that interests me extraordinarily. Analytical Psychology (or as it is now called: Complex Psychology) is deeply rooted in Europe, in the Christian Middle Ages and, in the last analysis, in Greek philosophy. The connecting link that eluded me for so long has now been found, it is alchemy, as Silberer already correctly suspected. Sadly he broke his neck on rational psychologism.

. . . .

The "Culture Jews" are always en route to being "non-Jews"; you are completely right, the route does not go from the good to the better, but first downhill to historical actuality. I routinely draw the attention of most of my Jewish patients to the fact that they are self-evidently Jews. I would not do this if I had not so frequently seen Jews who imagined that they were something else. To such as these "being Jewish" is a form of personal insult.

I have heard of Westmann's essay but have not yet read it. I'm told it is *very good*. Your disparaging assessment is valuable to me as is your very positive conviction that the Palestinian soil is essential to Jewish individuation. How does the fact that the Jew in general has lived in other countries than in Palestine for *much longer* relate to this? Even Moses Maimonides preferred Cairo (Fostat) even though he had the possibility of living in Jerusalem.

Is it then that the Jew is so accustomed to being a non-Jew that he requires the Palestinian soil *in concreto* in order to be reminded of his being Jewish? I find it hard to comprehend a soul which has grown up in no soil. [APE, 18J, pp. 118–119]

On 30 January 1936, Neumann wrote:

> I do not even believe that Palestinian soil is so important for the Jew but it will become so if ever this soil absorbs sufficient human beings to be a true ancestral soil once again. Certainly the Jews have lived much longer in other countries but without the contact to the soil that was not accessible to them due to their being rooted in the Torah. Now that this foundation of the law is fractured, and I see in Hasidism the revolution of this fracturing, we must come to a new beginning via a regression to the soil, if at all. Only now that the 2,000-year-old law in its role as an artificial psychospiritual root soil is broken, is Palestine starting to become relevant and the history of the spiritual productive time is fused with this. Both Maimonides and Philo are in fact assimilated Jews—but they could afford to be—because the root soil of the law made them independent of mere natural national limitations to which we had to return after the emancipation, while consciously repudiating our sole cosmopolitan supranational stance.
>
> . . . When I was with you back then, you said to me "Widen your horizons!" To a certain degree I think this has happened. I would have to contradict you today if you said to me that, for me, it was all about the Jewish problem, it is beginning to be about me, the Jewish aspect is the obvious location of my debate. Europe, Asia, Primitives, there the Jewish part is a small point, albeit an important one for me, and, as I still believe, also one of general importance. [APE, 19N, pp. 120–121]

In the summer of 1936, Neumann met Jung in Zurich, and they worked together for a while. It was to be their last meeting until 1947, after the Second World War. In this year (1936) there was a certain easing in the anti-Semitic propaganda and the persecution of the Jews in Germany. National Socialist Germany was preparing for the Olympic Games in Berlin and making efforts to appear more moderate.

Neumann was not able to persuade Jung to express criticism of the Nazis and their racist, anti-Semitic policies either in words or in writing.

Neumann returned to Tel Aviv, and there is no evidence of any further correspondence between them until the beginning of 1937.

On 20 January 1937, Neumann writes:

> Today I would like only to send you a short greeting to maintain the
> feeling that I have not lost the contact with you. The time in Zurich
> was eminently fruitful, the development initiated then is ongoing,
> even if it has been pushed into the background by a strong—i.e.,
> therefore welcome—professional demand. This development, to-
> gether with the work for my course: Soul problems of the modern
> Jew, stand at the center for me and the work on the book on which
> you have already given a mortgage is resting externally at the mo-
> ment, precisely because internally it has entered a new phase that I
> would like to wait upon.
>
> As you will be able to imagine, I had a mountain of inquiries, but
> I will not bother you with them but simply wait until the answers
> have formed themselves for myself.
>
> Things are fairly good with us. The situation is however quite
> dark. Where is light today. [APE, 22N, pp. 127–128]

Kristallnacht

On 10 November 1938, an organized anti-Jewish pogrom took place throughout Germany. All Jewish businesses were boycotted and hundreds of synagogues were set on fire. Thousands of Jews were beaten in the street, humiliated and abused; many were murdered, and thousands were sent to concentration camps. The Nazi hooligans smashed the shop windows of Jewish businesses, and the streets in every German town were covered in shards of glass. This terrible night is known as *Kristallnacht*. A tremendous fear gripped all Jews in the Third Reich.

Neumann wrote to Jung on 5 December 1938, shortly after *Kristallnacht*:

> Since I have written you such a large number of unwritten letters, I am resolving—now that is it doubly difficult—to finally get around to writing to you for real. I don't know if you can imagine how difficult it is today to maintain inner contact with someone like you who has inevitably been touched at best once by the events that are affecting us Jews. It is fully obvious and natural to me to know you live on a completely different plane from ours. Yes, I must say, it is almost a comfort to me to know that your age, if one might put it this way, has removed you some degrees from these horrific world events.
>
> On the other hand, this naturally impedes access a little, for I am most deeply convinced one should not bother you too much, as you, as I know and daily experience for myself, are already "fully immersed," as you once put it, in this world through your practice. Despite all this, it is a necessity for me to write to you once again if only to preserve the feeling that there is still a piece of Europe left, even for a Jew. [APE, 27N, p. 139]

Neumann's disappointment about Jung's lack of interest becomes obvious in this letter, as do his almost despairing efforts to hold on to his positive relationship to Jung. His hope of Jung's serious engagement and immersion in Jewish matters remained unfulfilled as did the hope that Jung—in response to the terrible *Kristallnacht*—would speak out unequivocally against the persecution of the Jews.

Even after *Kristallnacht*, which entailed such terrible attacks on Jews and their businesses in the German Reich, Neumann continues his defense of Jung. It is, for him, "fully obvious and natural" that Jung lives "on a completely different plane," and he is deeply convinced that "one should not burden [Jung] too much," and that he "has inevitably been touched at best once by the events [*Kristallnacht*] that are affecting us Jews."

He makes great efforts to continue feeling connected to Jung and to maintain the feeling that even for a Jew like Neumann "there is still a piece of Europe left." Jung represented this good piece of Europe to which Neumann is so attached. Neumann understands Jung and forgives him. He cannot afford to lose his last hold on Europe. He retains his strong sense of belonging to Europe, which treats its Jews so appallingly.

Kristallnacht was the worst pogrom in the modern age. It exceeded all previous instances of anti-Jewish persecution in its scope, in its ferocity, and in its Germany-wide organized planning. Despite this, the majority of Jews in Germany and in other European countries were not aware of an intent toward actual annihilation and could not believe in a catastrophe of such colossal dimensions. Neumann felt the impending catastrophe in his bones, foresaw the destruction of whole sections of the Jewish people. Only a few could foresee this in 1938. In his unshakeable faith, he regarded the approaching crisis and catastrophe as something that would call forth new strengths in the Jewish people:

> Despite all this, I have too great a debt of gratitude to this nation to be able to identify this simply as the symptoms of its schizophrenic episode. Added to this is the fact that I believe that these entire events will be, in brief, the salvation of Judaism, while at the same time I'm clear that I do not know if I will be among the survivors of this upheaval or not. The enormous extraversion of Judaism that

has led it to the brink of its grave will be cut off with the inexorable consistency of our destiny, and the terrible state of emergency that has gripped the entire people and will continue to do so will inevitably force the inner source energies to be called either into action or to their peril. It is both as clear to me that we will not be wiped out, as it is also that immeasurable numbers of us must perish in the process. And to watch this from the sidelines is a terrible torture. The reports that crowd in on one on a daily or hourly basis, and, sadly, the reports of eyewitnesses, make one glad to experience firsthand the terrible propensity of human beings to dissociate from overwhelmingly bad feelings. [APE, 27N, p. 140]

The letter ends on an optimistic note:

Thus, the full uncertainty about any future and yet still having the feeling of being in the right place gives me—at least now and again—a remarkably paradoxical inner confidence, from which I believe that there could be a new, lively beginning in the individual and in the collective. And exactly because what has been experienced by the individual has such a strong connection with that experienced collectively and repeatedly with what has been historically effective, this connection between the most individual and the ancient has something strong and almost joyful about it. [APE, 27N, p. 143]

In his postscript, he asks Jung again to engage more with Jewish development and awaits Jung's reference:

P.S. By the way, is it true that the dreamer in "Dream Symbols" and "Psychology and Religion" is a Jew? Will you publish anything on the specifically Jewish features of this development or do you see nothing specific about it. E.g., The "voice." And what about "Jewish material"? If you can say something about this, I would of course be very grateful. [APE, 27N, pp. 143–144]

Jung's reply to Neumann's letter was written on 19 December 1938. It was a speedy reaction:

You must not imagine that I have retreated to the snow-clad heights, enthroned high above world events. I am right in the thick of it and am following the Palestinian question on a daily basis in the newspapers, and think often of my acquaintances there who have to live in this chaos. When I was in Palestine in 1933, I was unfortunately able to see what was coming all too clearly. I also foresaw great misfortune for Germany, even quite terrible things, but when it then shows up, it still seems unbelievable. Everyone here is shocked to their core as it were by what is happening in Germany. I have a great deal to do with German refugees and am constantly occupied with accommodating all my Jewish acquaintances in England and America. In this way I am in constant contact with contemporary events.

. . . I think you must be very careful when evaluating your specifically Jewish experiences. While there are, for sure, specific Jewish traits in this development, it is at the same time a general one that is also happening among Christians. It is a question of a general and identical revolution of minds. The specifically Christian or Jewish traits have only a secondary meaning. So, for example, while the patient you asked about is a pure Jew raised as a Catholic, I could nowhere describe his symbolism, inasmuch as I could delineate it, as Jewish with any certainty beyond doubt, although certain nuances strike one as Jewish occasionally. If I compare his material with my own or with that of many other academically educated patients, it is only the surprising consistency that strikes one, the difference is negligible. The difference between a typically Protestant and a Jewish psychology is especially small when contemporary events are taken into consideration. The whole problem is itself of paramount importance for humanity that is why individual and racial differences only play a small part. All the same, I can imagine very well that among Jews who live in Palestine the immediate impact of the environment brings the chthonic and old-Jewish into view. It seems to me as if anything specifically Jewish as well as specifically Christian could be best discovered in the way and form that unconscious material is assimilated by the subject. In my experience the resistance of the Jews to this seems more obstinate and thus the defensive effort seems to be much more vehement. But this is nothing more than a purely subjective impression. [APE, 28J, pp. 145–146]

The Second World War

In September 1939, the German army attacked Poland and thus began the Second World War. Following the invasion of Poland and its
division between Nazi Germany and the Soviet Union, the war fronts
calmed down. A cessation in hostilities lasted several months. Italy had,
at that point, not yet joined the war, and Hitler was quietly preparing
his Blitzkrieg against Belgium and Holland with the intention of in-
vading France and taking Paris. He pulled this off in June 1940.

In this crucial period, Neumann wrote to Jung on 15 November
1939:

> Two things are colliding in me that cannot easily be reconciled, the
> one namely the consciousness of belonging to a dying people, and
> the other is the knowledge that something new is emerging—not
> Palestine—that is quite secondary—and that I am co-responsible
> for this. That this new thing should be done precisely to the im-
> possible object,—to the Jews—seems to me to be a paradox that
> strikes me as really Y.H.W.H.-like and Jewish. Please do not mis-
> understand me, I don't mean anything to do with chosenness or the
> prophetic, indeed it seems to me that it is precisely the sacrifice of
> these principles that is what we face today and that is so difficult for
> me. [APE, 29N, pp. 148–149]

Neumann is referring to Jung's letter of 19 December 1938, and
continues:

> In the meantime, I have also recognized that Jewish symbolism—
> at least that of Western Jews—is consistent with that of European
> people, that here something secular is taking place. Of course, I

knew this before, but the problem of the singularity of the Jews would have been simpler if a specific symbolism could have been demonstrated. [APE, 29N, p. 149]

In another section, he writes:

You see, dear Professor Jung, if I may interweave a very personal confession here, I do not believe in it, everything speaks against it, and I am so tired of the Jews and the Jewish—and every free minute and every thought belongs to these subjects, and I must protect myself from being completely swallowed up by this work. I am after all no "ignoramus," and Moses identification, prophet identification, etc. are not unknown facts to me. But, you see, my position toward Judaism is extremely revolutionary and even my attempt to create the continuity through to the modern Jewish person from the openness to revelation of antiquity via the inner Hasidic revolution is, as I of course will know myself, a new interpretation—how can I help myself in this paradox? [APE, 29N, p. 149]

Here we can see Neumann's effort to come to grips with areas where he really was no expert, areas related to Jewish history and Judaism. Neumann attempted to understand these Jewish problems and to interpret them with the intellectual tools and in the spirit of Jungian analytical psychology.

This effort was difficult and frustrating. Jung was insufficiently interested or perhaps not sufficiently qualified to pull Neumann out of the dilemmas and the problems which so troubled him at that time or to be helpful to him in that way.

At the end of this letter is another section that is quite different:

One more remark about Dr Stern. Without question, the devil has stirred things up there, the affair has taught me a great deal, also about myself. Anyway, the fact that he has become a passionate Freudian with all the accessories in the meantime confirms to me that his analysis with me was abysmal, but it has also shown me that my skepticism toward him that he did not "experience" and realize the contents was not completely incorrect. [APE, 29N, p. 153]

Neumann, the faithful Jungian, writes:

> I understand that one cannot always reach Jung from Freud,
> but to regress from Jung to Freud seems to me to be a moral
> defect, perhaps I am wrong, or better said to correspond to
> a Jewish-destructive nature. Anyway. My complex to feel too
> responsible still exists in any case, at least in part. [APE, 29N,
> p. 153]

On 16 December 1939, Jung wrote to Neumann:

> We are naturally very impacted by the immediate danger of war
> in our own land but for the time being everything is on hold.
>   In my lectures I am dealing with the Eastern orientation
> linked with yoga philosophy and the Western orientation
> linked to the Ignatian Spiritual Exercises. [APE, 30J, p. 155]

It can be clearly seen here that business as usual prevails; everything is
continuing more or less normally for Jung as a neutral Swiss citizen.
It was only after the beginning of the Second World War that Jung
finally gave up his position as president of the International (German)
Medical Society for Psychotherapy, which then ceased to exist.

The last letter from Neumann during this troubled time is from 11
May 1940:

> I hope very much that the contact with you, dear Professor, will not
> be interrupted, even through the passage of time; I am pretty much
> out on a limb and know very well that my work on the Jewish is very
> incomprehensible and untimely even for the Jews. All the more im-
> portant, then, is "Zurich" if I may call it something so impersonal
> when I mean something so personal. It is not so much about con-
> sensus as about the feeling of solidarity beyond what is different, of
> this you may be sure. [APE, 31N, pp. 156–157]

For the remainder of the Second World War and until the fall of 1945,
no letters between Neumann and Jung are extant.

After the War

It is difficult to believe that Neumann did not make contact with Jung immediately after the end of the war, and it is very likely that other letters have gone astray. The surviving correspondence begins again with a letter from 1 October 1945:

> The years in between in which I did not dare to write to you so as not to endanger you were no small thing. I very much hope that you, your family, and all individuals close to you have withstood this time without serious damage, inside or out. Fate has wrapped a tight bow around us, we are healthy and are working, and all close family members of my wife and myself managed to get out in time. That means a great deal and yet in such a time as ours is not very conclusive.
>
> I would like to briefly update you about myself. I can well imagine how you are being showered with updates from all over the world, but the contact to you and Miss Wolff is—even symbolically—the most precious thing, but also the only thing that is left to me of Europe. . . .
>
> . . . After I had completed the large work on Jewish antiquity— on the Soul History of the Jew—(it is now obsolete and only use-able as source material), I wrote a book on the psychological meaning of Hasidism for the modern Jew, which I still stand by. But then, after I had arrived at my current internal state, the Jewish problem and the work on it was ended as far as I was concerned, precisely at a time when it was becoming palpable in the world in an indescribably horrific way. I, meanwhile, was coming back to "pure" psychology. Firstly in essays and lectures from which I took

the liberty of sending you the larger work on *Depth Psychology and a New Ethic.* . . .

. . . .

You see, dear Professor, I am writing nothing about the times, nothing about Palestine. My inner dialectic indicates the only possible path for me. At these times, the general human condition moves me and this only. How else could one bear it. This "passionate intensity," if I may say so, makes life meaningful for me. And although I often check this out in myself, it does not seem to be a flight from the reality of the day. My practical work extends into this everyday reality, perhaps my other work will also do in future. The fact that, on the whole, I live in such an insular way here I regard as a requirement for my development and my work, which I must accept. I do not know where in the world I could have gone on working and maintaining my family in the last decade as I have been able to here. Much here is dangerous, absurd, and almost unbearable, but everything remains comprehensible at the same time, all too comprehensible. [APE, 33N, pp. 159–160, 163]

During the war years, Neumann worked a great deal on his first two books and was able to complete them. He sent Jung the first chapter of his work *The Origins and History of Consciousness* for his evaluation and critique. A letter from 4 June 1946 is enclosed with his manuscript:

In the last post I have sent you the first section of my book on the archetypal stages of the development of consciousness, which deals with the psychology of myth. The second section will follow very soon; I am just rewriting some elements of it. As you can imagine, this work is very important to me and I would like to publish this work this time. I think it is now ready to come out. The isolation of my existence in Palestine is probably greater than you imagine, and I fear a part of the deficiencies of which I was fully conscious on sending the manuscript to you has to do with this basic fact of my life. I have virtually no opportunity of discussing any scientific matters with peers, and this may be evident. [APE, 35N, p. 166]

Later he mentions a dream in which Jung says to him:

> "I would like to eat some more fruit with you." This sentence got
> into me in its own or in my own way, and independently of the com-
> plexity of its meaning, it has been a strong incentive for me. For, as
> paradoxical as it may be, it was a challenge to me, and for me, the
> book is a fruit, which, I am sending you herewith "to eat." [APE,
> 35N, p. 168]

Jung replies on 5 August 1946:

> I must not keep you waiting any longer, although I am by no means
> finished with all the reading you have sent me. In particular, your
> *magnum opus* gives me much to do. I am especially impressed by the
> clarity and precision of your formulations. I must tarry with any
> further impressions and ask you for corresponding patience. You
> can hardly imagine how overloaded with work I am, predominantly
> with letters. . . . The situation here is extremely difficult and every-
> thing is uncertain. While we are still living on our cultural island as
> before, everything around us is nothing but destruction, physically
> as well as morally. To do something reasonable oneself, you have to
> close your eyes. Germany is indescribably rotten. Letters I receive
> from there are, with a few exceptions, part childish, part obstinate,
> part hysterical, which convinces me more than everything that my
> diagnosis of the state of the German psyche was correct. . . .
> The situation in Palestine seems to be very difficult. The new age
> is announcing itself with endless birth pains. [APE, 37J, pp. 171–173]

It was the time of conflict in Palestine against British rule as well as
of illegal activity by the Jewish underground movement, the Hagana,
against the white paper ruling which had banned the free immigration
of Jewish Holocaust survivors to Palestine and had kept to a mini-
mum the number of immigration certificates. There were attacks on
the British police and military, carried out by the Jewish underground
movements Etzel and Lechi, as well as illegal immigration from Europe to Palestine, organized and led by the Hagana. The radical anti-
British terror underground movements attacked English police and

soldiers with acts of terror, and many were killed or injured. In the Jewish community in Palestine, the Yishuv, the atmosphere was very tense and there were great concerns about the future.

Jung's letter on 21 April 1947 is very kind and full of respect about Neumann's manuscripts:

> I asked you in my earlier letter whether you would be willing to have your manuscript printed here—I mean your great book. If you wish to publish it in this form, I would gladly recommend it to my publisher, Rascher. By the way, I have already hinted at this to him. In this book you have done a great deal better than I have and you have further developed much, where I got stuck in the difficulties of beginnings. I must tell you more about this—God willing. [APE, 42J, p. 181]

Neumann writes, on 23 April 1947, a letter that likely crosses Jung's in the mail:

> With great pleasure, I gather from Adler's letter that you like my book, that you want to offer it to Rascher and are even willing to write an introduction for him—and for me. It goes without saying that I am exceptionally pleased about this, and especially, as you can imagine, about the introduction, and I am not only in agreement but, far beyond that, I am most gratefully obliged to you. For I know what each new additional demand means for you that diverts you from the "main business," your own work.
>
> . . . .
>
> I am just revising the *Ethic* that you have also now read and that you also like—which I am very pleased about—because it has become too abstract and I feared it would be rather too "philosophical" for you. [APE, 43N, p. 183]

On 30 April 1947, Jung wrote a further letter:

> The things one reads in the papers about Palestine are not pleasant, for sure, but life elsewhere in Europe (with very few exceptions) is also not very pretty. I can't ward off a certain deep pessimism. [APE, 44J, p. 185]

On 24 May 1947, Neumann writes:

> The political is not as bad as it sounds and is made to sound, but
> bad enough. Your pessimism is, I fear, all too justified. But apart
> from the stark isolation,—where would it be better?—the life here
> is nice and healthy for the children. It is better for them to grow up
> in freedom among Jews, everywhere the "end" is uncertain. [APE,
> 49N, p. 192]

In the next three letters (two from Jung to Neumann and one from
Neumann to Jung), they have a discussion about the *castration complex*,
a term Neumann had made use of and which Jung had rejected.
Jung wrote on 1 July 1947:

> Having read your first volume, the only troubling terminology to
> strike me was that of the "castration complex." I consider the use
> of this term to be not only an aesthetic error, but also an erroneous
> overvaluation of the sexual symbolism. . . . The expression "castra-
> tion complex" is, to my taste, much too concretistic and therefore
> one-sided, . . . [APE, 52J, p. 195]

Neumann's reply from 8 July 1947:

> You can imagine how I pleased I was about your letter letting me
> know that Rascher has accepted my book. What is more, I am really
> touched by the active engagement you are showing toward me and
> my productions. . . .
>
> . . . .
>
> But now to the other important point of your letter, the objection
> to the "castration complex" terminology. You will excuse me if I
> elaborate at length here, but it is a matter for substantial discussion.
>
> Firstly, it goes without saying that I am in full agreement with
> you in this as we must avoid "everything that would amount in the
> end to allowing psychic events to appear as a derivative of a specific
> instinct." You write: "I consider this term not only an aesthetic er-
> ror but also an erroneous overestimation of the sexual symbolism.
> . . . The expression 'castration complex' is, for my taste, much too
> concretistic and therefore too one-sided."

I have looked through the first section once again in response to this and I would like to make the following remarks:

1) That the term castration as it is implemented and employed can hardly be misunderstood in a concrete way.

2) That I—up till now—have found no term that could replace it, the reasons for this I will explain.

3) That—and why—the "archetype of sacrifice" in connection with the first section does not express what is meant by the castration symbol.

All these possibly relevant arguments change nothing in regard to the fact that you believe that my remarks could be misunderstood in this manner; the question is, whether this is helped by an annotation. [APE, 53N, pp. 197–198]

On 19 July 1947, Jung writes:

I cannot repudiate the justification of "castration complex" terminology and even less its symbolism, but I must take issue with "sacrifice" not being a symbol. In the Christian sense it is even one of the most significant symbols. . . . Could one say *castration symbol* instead of castration complex, to be on the safe side? Or castration *motif* (like incest motif)?

You still have to gain experience for yourself as far as being misunderstood goes. The possibilities exceed all terminology. Perhaps you had better insert a short explanation in the text on the negative and the positive aspect of the symbol and, indeed, right at the beginning where you speak of the castration complex.

I hope very much that it will be possible for you to come to Switzerland. At the moment I am in my tower on the Obersee enjoying my holidays, which were most urgently needed. Our club wants to start a "C. G. Jung Institute for Complex Psychology." The preparations are already underway. [APE, 54J, pp. 202–203]

A Visit to Switzerland

O n 21 July 1947, Neumann writes to Jung:

This last year brought me renewed and deepened contact with you and your lively interest, and I can only hope that the next years and my work will take further what has begun to be a great enrichment for me. I do hope that you know how much your interest means to me, and what a necessary affirmation it is for me in an intellectual situation that often comes dangerously close to splendid isolation.

I hope still that we will soon be able to speak to you in person. . . .

Here, it is beginning to be very unsettled again, the future is very bleak here as it is everywhere, and it will be difficult for us to leave the children on their own in Palestine while we are in Switzerland. [APE, 55N, p. 204]

In the autumn of 1947, Neumann visited Switzerland for the first time since the war and met with Jung after a separation of eleven years. He presented him with his first two completed works: *Depth Psychology and a New Ethic* and *The Origins and History of Consciousness*. Jung was very impressed with these manuscripts and promised Neumann that he would help get them published with Rascher Verlag, who published his own works. He also helped him with contacts at the Bollingen Foundation in America, and thanks to Jung, Neumann made the acquaintance of Mrs. Fröbe-Kapteyn. Fröbe-Kapteyn organized the annual Eranos conferences in Ascona, to which important thinkers were invited to lecture. She invited Neumann to give a lecture the following year, 1948, on the theme of mystical man.

Shortly after Neumann had returned to Palestine from his very productive and successful visit to Jung, the United Nations determined that Palestine should be divided into Jewish and Palestinian states. The Arabs rejected the partition, and thus began the bloody events that developed into Israel's war of independence and led to the founding of the state of Israel. Neither Jung nor Neumann referred to these political events in their correspondence. Both were deeply immersed in their work. There are scarcely any observations in their correspondence concerning the important events taking place at that time in Palestine (Israel).

On 27 September 1947, Neumann wrote to Jung:

> I have much to thank you for from my stay in Europe, not only for your time that you gave to me and for your efforts with Rascher to which I attribute "substantially" the fact that he has taken on my book and *Ethic*.
>
> I had the impression of being strongly accepted and permitted into your midst and I very well have this to thank for the fact that now the central question—which I never actually asked you and which is also difficult to ask—seems to me, in hindsight, to have been answered. It is like in the—rationally hard to grasp—Hasidic stories where the Zaddik knows the question already and answers it in his sermon or in his conversation. But this is precisely one of the "last things" which I had to ask and it has become almost "unaskable," now that a new window, if not even a door has been opened to me once again.
>
> If the significance of my rather isolated self-sufficiency in Palestine has also become very clear to me once again, precisely because of Zurich, you will therefore understand how terribly much the possibility of meeting with you means and must mean. [APE, 58N, p. 207]

On 17 December 1947, he writes:

> But you will understand that after the holidays, my practice demanded my full attention first of all, and then the corrections of *Ethic*, the preparation of the great book, course preparations and,

not least, political events have very much laid claim to me. [APE, 59N, p. 209]

He goes on to criticize the Zurich Jungians:

> I think the Zurichers could easily do some more work. Analytical psychology must not be allowed to become a secret doctrine; to some degree it is this inevitably anyway anywhere that it seeks to grasp the essential secret of the psychical. But it means that the possible reach of analytical psychology is curtailed in a dangerous way if even the younger colleagues behave as if—you will forgive my malice—only the third half of life has any significance for humanity. [APE, 59N, p. 212]

Jung replies to this promptly on 8 January 1948:

> I fully appreciate what you argue in respect of the journal. Up till now, the difficulty has been with the staffing of it. There were and are too few active people available, and if something like this is to be initiated, we must be certain that someone very responsible will devote themselves to it so that something decent comes out of it. Everything has been so delayed by the war. We are only gradually starting to implement a plan of action that we should really have started years ago. Once the institute gets going and documents are published, then the next point on the action plan will be the journal. But for this, we must have assembled the necessary team. We can only expect real participation from you, from Switzerland, from America, and a bit from Holland. The English are rapidly going daft, and Germany is at ground zero to such a degree that one does not know at all what is going to happen there. France and Italy are not even in the picture as they are at least 50 years behind. As far as the Zurichers are concerned—you are completely right: they are still quite asleep. In this regard, I hope the institute will have an educative function and will awaken people out of this dream state.
>
> I read with great apprehension the news about Palestine in our newspapers and brood on ways and means of ever getting you out of this hornets' nest. [APE, 60J, p. 215]

On 24 January 1948, Neumann writes:

> Slowly it is getting so uncomfortable here because of the British
> betrayal that one cannot fail to see what will come out of it all. As a
> minor side issue, the post is in chaos. [APE, 62N, p. 217]

On 3 April 1948, he writes:

> There is not much new to report from me. The practice that has
> become a bit—not a lot—smaller—(nearly everyone under 35 has
> been called up)—is, pleasingly, giving me rather more time during
> which I have for sure enough to do. Since the danger of being with-
> out any postal connection looms once again, even with Switzerland
> by the way . . . [APE, 63N, p. 219]

And later in the same letter:

> I am sure you will speak to Dr. Braband; as I have the fully un-
> grounded impression that she wishes to leave Palestine, I would
> like to urge you not to believe all the negative things she says—
> if she does so. She does not see the truly hellish shadow problem
> at all, not in micro or in macro, it seems to me. Possibly we will
> all perish from it—only we?—but it is terribly overwhelming
> to see how the acceptance of the shadow, earth and blood all
> belong together and how obviously, even today, the longing for
> roots and the offering up of blood sacrifices to the earth be-
> long together. The fact that one has the "evil eye" because one
> comprehends but is distanced from it does not make it easier,
> especially as one can only do anything about it in individual
> work and otherwise one must be silent for the time being. [APE,
> 63N, p. 220–221]

A New Ethic and "Mystical Man"

What actually occupied Neumann in the years 1947–1948 were his first two works. The book *Depth Psychology and a New Ethic* tackles the values of Judeo-Christian ethics. The old ethic as Neumann defined it requires repression. The repressed evil is then projected outward, onto the other, the scapegoat. Thus develops a disastrous, unbridgeable split between good and evil. The repressed evil is the shadow, and the fact that it is split off from the conscious personality is dangerous. Neumann wrote that the shadow must be integrated into the personality. While this is difficult and painful, it is less dangerous and destructive than the old repressed ethic.

When this book, with its revolutionary thesis, was published in complacent, bourgeois, Protestant Switzerland, it became a great sensation and triggered a wave of opposition and criticism in that country, especially in Jung's closer circles.

The next letters bear witness to the stormy emotions which followed the publication of the book and put the relationship between Jung and Neumann to a severe test. Neumann makes the greatest of efforts to safeguard his good relationship with Jung.

The war of independence was continuing, and finally there is a reference to this in a letter from Neumann to Jung on 12 July 1948. He writes about the difficulties in Israel arising from the war and mentions Egyptian bombing, which had completely destroyed a house opposite Neumann's apartment:

> It is uncertain whether I will get the exit permit from here. I hope it will be OK. Everyone under 41 is in the army, I am 43. If, as I believe, there will soon be a cease fire, I could then come. As long as we're being mindlessly bombed all over the place, I am unable to

make the decision to travel. Yesterday a bomb dropped next to us, it can happen on every corner and at any time—to travel in this is impossible. But I still hope that it will work. Even so, I will come alone and perhaps for a short time, but all this will sort itself out. [APE, 66N, p. 226]

He hopes it will still be possible for him to go to Switzerland, but he is more occupied with intellectual than with practical matters. He writes:

I will, for sure, always be on the margins in Palestine, sorry—in Israel, even on the most extreme margin, and almost on the outside, but here, there is no protected Judaism as an optimal state, and indeed a dangerous but healthy shadow development that at least makes a healthy and creative nation possible. For me, a paradoxical but apparently beneficial situation. [APE, 66N, p. 227]

Jung replies on 17 August 1948:

I finished reading your lecture yesterday. I can only express my admiration to you for the manner and style in which you have mastered your difficult task. It has turned into a quite excellent representation, as clear as it is thorough, of the problem of the mystic. This has never before been captured in such an extensive way and in such depth as in your work. [APE, 69J, p. 232]

On 13 November 1948, Neumann writes:

Even if I am generally glad to be here and not in Zurich for many other reasons, envy still naturally grips me when I see the Zurichers referring to manuscripts of yours that are still unknown to me. . . .

    Here things are going well for me and for all of us, with plenty of work, and we are all quite optimistic. Without the world noticing, something remarkable is happening here—and despite everything—it is positive. [APE, 71N, pp. 234–235]

In September 1948, Neumann went to Switzerland and gave his

first Eranos lecture at Ascona. His lecture, "Mystical Man," was very well received, and from this year on he was a permanent and very popular speaker at every annual Eranos conference until his death in 1960.

It can be assumed that when Neumann met with Jung, he received endorsement and assurances that Jung would support him, but as it later emerged, this support aroused great criticism and much opposition.

Jung's letter to Neumann on 10 December 1948 illustrates this quite clearly:

> Your text on the *Ethic* has appeared here and is already stirring up the dust and, indeed, in such a way, that it might come to my having to speak out about it. At the institute the question has arisen whether it would now be wise, given the circumstances—and taking advantage of your kind willingness—to bring out your book as part of the institute's series of publications. The fear exists that future discussions would be prejudiced by this, and that the institute would be defining itself by certain formulations, even if only morally, or that it would be giving the appearance of doing so. [APE, 72J, p. 236]

Here, Jung adds a sentence for which Neumann never forgave him: "A small institute, which still stands on weak legs, must not risk too many opponents. (Side glances to university and church!)" [APE, 72J, p. 236]

Jung writes further:

> I have reread your text and again had a very strong response to it, and I am certain that its effect will be like that of a bomb. Your formulations are brilliant and of incisive sharpness; they are therefore challenging and aggressive, an assault troop in an open field, where there was nothing to be seen in advance, unfortunately. Naturally the opponent concentrates his fire on the unprotected troops. It is precisely the obviously bold but unambiguous formula that is most vulnerable because it has an unprotected side. [APE, 72J, p. 236]

Jung criticizes Neumann's lack of caution, but he also encourages him: "One cannot fight a war without losses, and one gets nowhere with a static equilibrium" [APE, 72J, p. 236]. Jung is enthusiastic and writes:

> Even the title *"New" Ethic* is a trumpet cry: aux armes, citoyens! We will get some poison gas in the nose and some dirt on the head. In Tel Aviv you risk occasional Egyptian bombs for it.
>   I am not quarrelsome, but I am strident by nature and therefore I cannot conceal from you my secret pleasure. [APE, 72J, p. 237]

Jung, who was seventy-three years old at this time and the head of the Jungian "establishment," acts honorably and responsibly to all external appearances, but in his personal letter he supports Neumann and signals to him in a mischievous way that he is enjoying the confusion and chaos that Neumann has created. Jung ends his letter:

> But I will have to act concerned and possibly exercise my duty as commandant of the fire brigade. Your writings will be a *petra scandali*, but also the powerful impetus for future developments. For this I am most deeply grateful to you. [APE, 72J, p. 237]

Jung was criticized for his support of Neumann and his views, which were considered extreme and unacceptable. He withdrew his support to some degree, and his stance became rather reserved.

On 12 January 1949, Jung wrote a letter to Dr. Jürg Fierz, the editor of the Swiss newspaper *Die Weltwoche*. This letter reads:[6]

> Above all you must realize that I am not in the habit of interfering with my pupils. I have neither the right nor the might to do that. They can draw such conclusions as seem right to them and must accept full responsibility for it. There have been so many pupils of mine who have fabricated every sort of rubbish from what they took over from me. I have never said that I stand "uncompromisingly" behind Neumann. There is naturally no question of that. It should be obvious that I have my reservations.
>   If you want to understand Neumann properly you must be realize

that he is writing in the spiritual vacuum of Tel Aviv. Nothing can come out of that place for the moment except a monologue. He writes as he fancies.

Up until this point in his letter, Jung is quite reserved and critical. The turn in his attitude soon becomes clear and, out of his cool, rational, and balanced stance, another Jung appears who is enthusiastic and youthful in his disposition, a nonconformist, who does support Neumann. This is the Jung who rebelled against Freud. He writes:

> This is certainly provocative, but I have found that provocative books are not the worst, but they get under some people's skin who could not be reached in any other way.

And then follows:

> If I am commending his small book, it is mainly because it demonstrates what conclusion can be arrived at if one thinks through the ethical problem uncompromisingly to the end. One must bear in mind that Neumann is a Jew and consequently he only knows Christianity from the outside; and furthermore, one must be aware that it has been drastically demonstrated to the Jews that evil "is always projected."
>
> If I were to write about ethics, I would of course not at all express myself as Neumann does. But I am also not the Neumann who has been backed into a combative oppositional standpoint by an horrendous fate. It does not surprise me at all if he presents the world with a difficulty because of this which umpteen people must complain about, and I will not hold it against him either. I cannot regret it either if these so-called Christians are rather annoyed by it. They have richly deserved it. One always talks of Christian morality and I would like to see those who really follow it! Neumann is not being shown even the slightest understanding, let alone any talk of loving thy neighbor.

On 1 January 1949, Neumann replied to Jung's letter from 10 December 1948:

Your letter was as much a great joy as a surprise. I must admit to you that I in no way expected to cause a stir or even a scandal in the close-knit circle of Jung students with my *Ethic*. In my opinion I have only summarized, thought through to the end, and formulated in a way that cannot be misunderstood what you yourself have stated or implied countless times. It is absolutely fair enough that the emphasis of your interest did not exactly focus on the ethical consequences, but shifted more and more to the later phases of psychic development, and that seems to me to derive from your own development. You went through the weight of the ethical problematic in your time as student, friend, and opponent of Freud and then grew beyond it. But then the necessary polemic against Freud has caused a section of your students to turn a blind eye to how much blood was spilled in this debate, and how your moral courage in separating from Freud perpetuated Freud's moral courage with which he set himself against his time. Indeed, you have personally emphasized over and over again—at least in many conversations with me—the significance of the moral stance of the "ego" and of the strength of the "ego," but, in your writing, this aspect is often less evident as is the obvious therapeutic aspect in general. My inner "consternation," to formulate it in an exaggerated way—about the condition of the Jung students in Zurich, now evidently to me at least, seems I fear, to be substantiated. If I found something amiss, for example, or not as it should be, there were only two reactions, either they said—in a highly satisfied way—yes, yes that is just the shadow, or they smiled in a rather superior way about my provincial attitude, which was thought not quite up to it simply because I made a value judgment about where one ought to allow the wisdom of the unconscious to prevail, beyond good and evil. But they seemed to me all too often to mistake the unconsciousness of the ego for the wisdom of the unconscious. [APE, 73N, pp. 238–239]

Neumann is indirectly taking Jung to task with his attack on his students at the Jung Institute. He adds sarcastically:

If pure ambition and casting side glances at both "university and church,"—and also power and money—belong to the foundations

of the C. G. Jung Institute, then one should let this institute be
eradicated, because it is, in fact, abusing your name and endan-
gering your life's work. You know, and I know all too well, that my
strong Mars tendency signifies a danger, but my heart rose when
you wrote to me that you have a "strident nature." I understand
most deeply that it can no longer be your task to get involved in the
battle of the day, and for God's sake please do not misunderstand
me and think that I am requesting a defense of *Ethic* or even of my
person, but I do request you—in your role as "fire brigade commandant"—not to extinguish too enthusiastically, where the fire,
that ancient cleansing method of humanity, could possibly eradi-
cate some filth. Some of the reservations against your teaching are
based on the unrevolutionary and all too bourgeois stance of your
students who always wish to anticipate the wisdom of the "third
half of life" before they have the struggles of the first behind them.
The synthetic and superior stance of your age, which contains the
opposites, conceals from your "heirs," who ogle at the so-called
treasures of this world and want to have everything at once, the
aggressive and revolutionary character of your work—and despite
everything—of your being. I do not wish to conceal from you that
it sometimes seems to me that you are yourself rather complicit
in this. I know that psychologists are not a "religious order," but I
do not understand fully how it can be that the necessary fourth is
the devil, and in the patronage of the institute can sit enemies of
this devil—legitimate and serious enemies. I confess even that I am
naïve enough to consider Mrs. Jacobi's Catholicism as offensive—
to put it unkindly etc., etc. Where's the "new ethic" now, you will
perhaps ask me, and you could say that what I am attacking, like
"Savonarola," is precisely one of their and your conclusions. But
I believe that is not the case. In my experience, this acceptance of
the fourth is, as the fine German language puts it, a "devilishly difficult" matter, and in no way so pleasant and easy a thing as, say, a
compromise. [APE, 73N, pp. 239–240]

Neumann goes on the offensive and writes to Jung, the Swiss:

You see, the neutral stance of Switzerland also has its risks alongside
all that is good. With the exception of you, of course, they have not

experienced the evil that has the whole world by the throat, and this is the bourgeois-ethical inadequacy that endangers your students.

. . . what frightens me is the absence of passion of the spirit that, for example, is suggested in your implied reaction to my text, everywhere seeking reassurances against the truth.

Of course there is nothing I would want less than to damage you or the institute and I can now assure you that I would respond positively to a request from the institute not to publish my book there. At the same time, though, I would like to assure you that my fervent efforts will continue to prove myself worthy of "the hate of the pussyfooters." [APE, 73N, pp. 240–241]

On 3 February 1949, Neumann received notice from the Jung Institute in Zurich that *Depth Psychology and a New Ethic* had not been included in its list of published Jungian works.[7]

Dear Colleague, As you have already know from Jung, due to the fierce public and private controversy which has arisen about your *New Ethic*, the question has been discussed in the Institute about whether it would be right to publish the "Origins and History of Consciousness" in the Institute's own series. After a comprehensive discussion in the Curatorium, we came to the decision that it would be better for the young Institute not to expose itself to too much fierce public controversy. For now, we would prefer to publish works which have the character of monographs on questions of Complex Psychology which require a better material and scientific underpinning. Therefore, it also seems to me personally right if your large comprehensive work appears as a publication in its own right, and I can thus understand the decision of the Curatorium to this effect. I hope that you will not have any difficulties with this and assure you that we are all very much looking forward to your book coming out. With best wishes, ever yours, C. A. Meier [APE, pp. 243–244, note 460]

On 10 February 1949, Neumann writes to Jung:

It is difficult to get my bearings in the Zurich games of shadows and to differentiate between the "being" and its shadow, and although I should now be an expert in the shadow, it remains difficult. . . .

I have been informed by the Curatorium of the institute that bears your name and whose president you are that it is not desirable that my book *The Origins and History of Consciousness* should be published as a publication of the institute. I had not sought this honor, but on the contrary, long after the contract with Rascher was agreed, I gave permission, post hoc, for the book to be taken on by the institute. At that time, following my good intuition, I immediately turned to you with the question regarding whether the institute was under your leadership and made my permission conditional on this (14 July 1948). I hereby lay aside this honor, as I have already communicated with you in my reply to your private letter, into the hands of those who have recalled it. [APE, 74N, pp. 243–244]

At the end of his spirited letter, Neumann writes:

I would like to call upon you—although I am perhaps not entitled to do so—as the "Commandant of the Fire Brigade" in the old biblical style: "Philistines be upon thee, Samson!"

For two reasons, however, I am grateful for the decision of the Curatorium even though it has cut me off once and for all from your institute and its representatives. It seems to me to be fatefully correct that my book and I myself have been expelled from your institute. On the outside, I find myself quite well and in the best of company, namely, in that of C. G. Jung, provided he is not president. So herewith I accept the honor, dear Professor, of representing the truth of your psychology in the world, for which there is no room in your institute.

The second reason—which I have seen with some consternation—is that the [new] Ethic is much less up to date than I had believed, as the simple values of the old ethic, e.g., integrity, the love of truth, and courage, are still unknown in the circles of people whom I considered to be representatives of the new ethic. So yet again, the church is correct to have banned me—and you—in the name of the institute. [APE, 74N, pp. 245]

Neumann closes his sharp letter with a painful observation:

> Do you recall the question, dear Professor, about why so few men come to you? It is not easy to accept the things you ask of us. Please imagine your own reaction if this had happened to you with one of your books at a Freudian Institute, moreover, in the case of a book for which Freud himself had written the foreword. But this example is wrong. That would not have been possible. [APE, 74N, pp. 245]

Jung replied on 29 March 1949:

> I can understand your annoyance but I had to marvel at your both mild and acquiescent reply in your last letter but one. I have concluded from this that it is not important to you anyway how your book is published. I have naturally communicated your previous response to Dr. Meier. Now, if you had protested immediately to the degree that you have done so in your recent letter, I would have attempted to push through my original intention of publishing your book in the series. You must understand my current situation somewhat: I have to try to operate under the current circumstances, but I would like to avoid the emergence of some sort of orthodoxy that pushes out other types of individuality. Since your clear reaction to my original proposal, I have now gone back to the Curatorium. [APE, 75J, p. 246]

On 6 April 1949, Neumann wrote a bitter letter to Jung:

> Your silence in response to both of my letters has rather unsettled me, but I thought perhaps you had too much to do and so I was only a little sad. Now I see—as I have received a letter from Miss Wolff today—that I have "fallen from grace" and that the court has turned away from me. That troubles me little, even if I am astonished to hear from Miss Wolff that all of a sudden my point of view "is not actually that of depth psychology" that had never even once occurred to me, to you, or to Miss Wolff—until recently. However, if I must now accept that you are angry with me or that your silence has arisen from your breaking off your relationship with me—I would in no way be prepared to put up with this. I am willing to defend *The*

New Ethic—which apparently no longer has any friends in Switzerland—in open battle against the whole institute, Protestants, Catholics, baptized Jews, unbaptized Jews, and even against Jungian analysts if any should show up, and I pledge to prove from the writings of C. G. Jung that my teaching is the real and unfalsified teaching of Holy Jungian Psychology that I believe myself to represent now, as ever, against friend and foe.

Who would have thought it! Never would I have thought that your droll warning that I had yet to experience how much one can be misunderstood would have to become a reality in this highly surprising way. May I quote you something from Miss Wolff's letter that shows the "revised" position? "You no longer seem to be on good terms with nature, hence with the unconscious and the inner laws of nature. Your old testament perspective is getting in your way. This is why it must indeed be a text on ethics." Dear Professor Jung—now tell me yourself,—it would be laughable if it did not make me cry. Here [in I.] one is indignant that I am so anti-Jewish, which I can understand, and all of a sudden one discovers—you must surely have vilified me—I am representing an old testament perspective in the *Ethic*. You see it has come to this, if you let them get away with casting "side glances at university and church" in "only" ethical matters. Why, for God's sake, do you not understand the danger that threatens you and us and your work if such things are possible.

Please believe me that this is not about me and not about "being right" and certainly not about an endorsement of me by the—as far as I'm concerned—not very authoritative Jung Institute. I will be able [and will have to] make my way without that also, but I don't want—through your covering of things with which you are yourself in no way identical—for it to now come out that yes means no and no means yes. Everything I have written is now supposed to be false because I have dared to exercise a critique of your technical position, because I, as has been shown, rightly do not believe that these things can be wielded technically or pragmatically. Of course, all this is happening—crazily—only to retrospectively reinforce your position "against" Neumann that, in my opinion was never intended as such by you. What intellectual disingenuous is all this! Can you not now at least understand from the outcome of this "affair" how justified my reaction is? I still dare to hope that if I am additionally roaring like a "lion," shaking my mane and not simply letting my coat be ruffled by holy and unholy dogs, that you must understand this as a "Fellow Lion."

I now have nothing more to say; I hope very much that this unfortunate, crazy, and ugly matter has not taken up your time and energy that you need for other things. I am anyway, now as ever, with and without *Ethic*, Your grateful, [APE, 76N, pp. 248–250]

Neumann is furious and hurt, but he attempts to differentiate between Jung and the "court," that is, Jung's close circle in Switzerland. He makes great efforts to preserve his good relationship with Jung.

Jung had promised to write introductions to both of Neumann's books, and he even sent drafts of his introductions, which were intended to be published in Neumann's books. But Jung was under pressure and was influenced by the opposition to the new ethic. He was accused of having a special relationship with and of showing favoritism to Neumann. In response he changed his opinion and was persuaded that he should be more reserved, at least outwardly.

In March 1949, Jung wrote a foreword to Neumann's *Depth Psychology and a New Ethic*:[8]

The problem is indeed a vital one. This may explain why the question of a new ethic is of such serious and urgent concern to the author, who argues his case with a boldness and passion well matched by his penetrating insight and thoughtfulness. I welcome this book as the first notable attempt to formulate the ethical problems raised by the discovery of the unconscious and to make them a subject for discussion.

This is only one section from a longer introduction, but there is no endorsement of the ideas expressed in this book.

Neumann was hurt, and on 9 April 1949, he wrote a letter of protest about the change from the enthusiastic version that Jung had written in May 1948 to the cautiously reserved version of March 1949. He writes:

An institute bearing your name may not permit itself to choose the term "promote" for a foreword from you, and it ought even less to imply that it has made a censorious revision to a foreword of yours, one written for a book that is absolutely not permitted to appear under its auspices. [APE, 77N, pp. 251]

This apparently rather pedantic letter is referring to the changes in the two versions, from a positive to a neutral evaluation. Neumann goes on:

For this is, of course, the background to the otherwise quite inappropriate communication of the Institute . . . "so you must let it come out as a book in its own right, with the foreword from Professor Jung which he will send you the final version of directly."

It is not about the fact that May '48 shone more favorably on me than April '49, nor about the qualifications to your endorsement of me that seem necessary to you. I have nothing to say about this, although the discrepancy between "creating a unified whole" and "woven his facts into a pattern" is monstrous. The second formulation leaves the question completely open as to whether these contexts are relevant, which the first implies with your all too kind emphasis.

My concerns are about the new inclusions, my bitterness about a change that is at the root of Dr. Meier's fear of a system that scared him off even in Ascona. When you formulated, for the first time, "buildings in which the empirical conceptual forms find their natural living space," you were under the influence of the book itself; "finding a living space," with the new addition about the personal equivalence and the exclusion of the "textbook sentence" from which I knew immediately that it would heap the enmity of Zurich upon me—that is a total distancing that perhaps is not intended by you in the way it now sounds. Now it sounds like this—to me: What can one do, there are simply some people who, for good or ill, cannot help creating a system and concocting hypotheses about it. Thank God there are other sorts of people too. Of course I am exaggerating. But it seems to me that the completely understandable qualification of your all too strong endorsement—which evokes no sort of "bitterness"—belongs to this. Now, all that remains is the qualification and the endorsement is dubious in decisive points.

I fear that your institute and Mrs. Jacobi, especially, will have to create an orthodoxy for the very reason that nothing of their own occurs to them, and you, dear Professor, will not be able to do anything about this. However, I promise you I won't let them put my back to the wall, as far as it is possible to me. I already know now that I am naturally a bad Jewish-intellectual student of yours, for whom the essential thing evades me. Hence my anger at the sentence in the disloyal letter from Miss Wolff that I quoted to you. I adhere to the sentence from Mrs. von Keller after the incident with Meier, which was the start of it all: Now you must go on your way like a rhino and not look to the left or the right. [APE, 77N, pp. 251–254]

In 1949, Jung's foreword was published in Neumann's book *The Origins and History of Consciousness*. Jung wrote:[9]

The author has requested me to preface his book with a few words of introduction, and to this I accede all the more readily because I found his work more than usually welcome. It begins just where I, too, if I were granted a second lease of life, would start to gather up the *disjecta membra* of my own writings, to sift out all those "beginnings without continuations" and knead them into a whole. . . . Thus forewarned and forearmed, a representative of the second generation can spot the most distant connections; he can unravel problems and give a coherent account of the whole field of study, whose full extent the pioneer can only survey at the end of his life's work.

This difficult and meritorious task the author has performed with outstanding success. He has woven his facts into a pattern and created a unified whole, which no pioneer could have done nor could ever have attempted to do.

On 16 July 1949 Neumann wrote on the occasion of Jung's seventy-fourth birthday:

Firstly I would like to wish you all the best for your birthday, and hope that your health and strength have been restored to you and to us all as in the last few years. You do know that I also hope to be able to see and speak with you personally—as much as indeterminable fate will allow. Alongside the surprising and rather sinister matter of the publications, the last year has bestowed on me, in compensation, so much that is personally unexpected and not easily digestible that my relationship with you, dear Professor Jung, is indeed the firmest link that ties me personally to Europe, despite everything. It goes without saying what this means as there is, for me, no other shore than the Occidental European one. [APE, 80N, p. 262]

Jung wrote to Neumann on 28 August 1949. He praised Neumann's lecture for the Eranos conference in 1949 and added the following observation:

Only—you have the tendency of characterizing the unconscious too pessimistically. It would be advisable to immediately place a positive remark after every negative one, otherwise one gets the impression of a catastrophic tragedy without grace from above. That would just not resonate with the experience: "that God helps the brave." [APE, 82J, p. 265]

The very different mentality is clearly evident here. On Neumann's side is the Jew after the Holocaust, who foresees the difficult dangers of the unconscious, like Freud, the Jew (Freud was also accused of being too pessimistic), and on the other side is Jung, the Swiss, who naively and optimistically believes that "God helps the brave."

Aftermath

The storm over Neumann's book *Depth Psychology and a New Ethic* abated, and in the course of time Neumann was accepted by the Jungians in Switzerland and even invited to teach at the institute and later to serve as director. Neumann, however, maintained his reserve toward the Jung establishment and protected and promoted his good relationship with Jung, with Jung's wife Emma, and with his colleague Aniela Jaffé.

In July 1950, Neumann writes a letter to Jung for his seventy-fifth birthday:

> You will understand how immensely difficult it is to write a birthday letter to you, and especially for your 75th. Such a day prompts me so urgently to reflect and to try to capture what the encounter with you has meant for my life and just how much your life per se has been growing in significance, quite independently from me—how could all this be expressed in a letter.
>
> In the autumn of '34, I came to you for the first time, then in '36 from Palestine and then finally, after 11 years and the war and many experiences, came the reunion with you in '47. That is a long stretch of life. Of course you don't know what it meant for me that I have always had the impression and retain it to this day, that in your eyes as well my work is meaningfully affiliated with yours . . . [APE, 83N, p. 266]

Later in the letter, Neumann writes:

> In this remote little country, which is diminutive, in many things narrow and barbaric, productive in much, and pregnant with the

future, I stand, inwardly of course, completely alone, with a decaying Europe at my back and a dangerously emergent Asia before me. Indeed, in this situation the reconnection with you has always been a vital support. [APE, 83N, p. 266]

And then, in what follows, Neumann's personal relationship with Jung can be clearly seen:

Many remarkable things have happened to me, and I have thus experienced much in other ways and forms, and with hindsight, I know that you have been my inner leader in it all. This has often been a comfort to me, especially as I experience much in a very different and contradictory way from you, as you know. In this way, far beyond these "incidents" and "frivolities," a transcendent sense of belonging to you has always remained inwardly apparent to me and it is possibly stronger than you imagine. [APE, 83N, p. 267]

It is interesting to read these lines from Neumann to Jung alongside a complaint from Jung in a letter to Freud of 3 December 1912, in which he wrote:[10]

If these blinkers were removed you would, I am sure, see my work in a very different light. As evidence that you—if I may be permitted so disrespectful an expression—*underestimate* my work by a very wide margin, I would cite your remark that "Without intending it, I have solved the riddle of all mysticism."

Jung's need to receive endorsement and recognition from Freud for his work was great and enduring, and for this reason it is especially painful to read Freud's indifference and criticism.

Just as Jung was generous to Neumann and not envious of him, Neumann was enthusiastic about Jung's work. In 1951 Neumann read Jung's work *Answer to Job*, and on 5 December 1951, he wrote to Jung:

Firstly it is a book that grips me deeply, I find it the finest and deepest of your books, and I should also say that it is actually no longer a "book." In a certain sense it is an argument with God, a concern

similar to that of Abraham when he argues with God because of
the downfall of Sodom. It is—for me personally—especially also an
argument against God who allowed 6 million of "His" people to be
killed, . . . [APE, 86N, p. 271]

But Neumann does not understand Jung's disregard of the Jewish in
his work, and he asks:

But then the confinement to the canonical books is still not comprehensible, why then do Gnosis and the Jewish Midrash not belong
here? Is it only about the Western image of God, you do mean the
general transformation of the image of God, but can one simply
leave out Asia? And if so, is it not even more the God-image of
Western humanity? [APE, 86N, p. 272]

Jung replied quickly, within a few weeks, to Neumann's letter. On 5
January 1952, he writes:

I thank you very much for your kind letter and the way you understand me. This compensates for 1,000 misunderstandings! You have
put your finger on the correct spot, one that is painful for me. [APE,
89J, p. 280]

On 28 February 1952, Jung wrote to Neumann: "I must let you
know in the proper way how much your *Amor and Psyche* pleased me.
It is brilliant,—and written with the keenest *sympathy*." [APE, 91J, p.
287]
Neumann's reply of 21 June 1952:

Now I am once again so much in your debt! Thanks for your last
letter, thanks for the *Job* and for the off-prints! I have wanted to
write for a long time but it wouldn't work. Firstly I was too much
wrapped up in myself and then in a work that I have been despair-
ingly grappling with. It was in fact supposed to become the Eranos
lecture, in the meantime I am writing more and more . . . . But there
is simply nothing to be done about it. A highly "meta-psychologi-
cal" thing, falling between all chairs of all faculties. But I had at least
to make the attempt, even if only perhaps for myself, of coming up

with a unified model that gives a place to all the phenomena that till now have been rattling around at the edge of our worldview. They are all things that have exercised and bothered me for years with links to the *Spirit of Psychology* . . . . [APE, 92N, p. 290]

In the following year and half, the letters exchanged were brief and the topics quotidian, as Jung was struggling with serious illness. The conversation was taken up again on 28 December 1953, when Neumann wrote:

> While I frequently detect with amazement how much by you has now been accepted by the Freudians without you noticing, I detect with the same amazement how the Jungians do not recognize me or do not wish to recognize me. I always recall then with pleasure your prophecy about *Origins*: You will see, they will not read you even once, but with time it will come. So I pat my leonine ambition ever reassuringly on the shoulder and comfort myself with the fact that production is still going well, which is after all the actual enjoyment of the matter, if one can call this thing enjoyment that on the other hand is an abominable torment.
>
> . . . . On the other hand, I must admit a mild horror grips me at the expanding pile of printed and written paper that rustlingly asserts a connection with me. It is truly a type of compulsion and addiction—I have been writing almost continuously since my twelfth, certainly since my sixteenth year—and while I also know that this is definitely part of my nature and, I hope, of my authentic life task, it sometimes seems to be a true paper hell. [APE, 97N, pp. 300–301]

Neumann ended his letter with a personal note:

> Besides that, I am on the verge of a writing wave and I am engaged in the solemn rites of resistance and the ultimate surrender to this wave. Are you familiar with anything like this yourself, or does this belong to my individual idiosyncrasies? [APE, 97N, p. 301]

Once again Neumann attempted to bring Jung closer to Judaism. On 24 January 1954, he wrote:

It pleases me hugely when research increasingly comes upon the Jewish origins of Gnosticism. I have always suspected this, already because of kabbalah, quite apart from myself. For me this is certainly also an primal position out of which originates the Christian in Judaism, which adheres so differently and so much more intimately to the person of Jesus than the church does and what has come out of that in Christendom. [APE, 98N, p. 303]

Jung responded quickly, on 30 January 1954:

I have penetrated quite far into your *Cultural Development* and will be able to read further as soon as the letter mountain that has collected during my absence is demolished.

I would acknowledge without further ado the description "Gnostic" if it were not a term of abuse in the mouth of a theologian. They accuse me of the same crime of which they make themselves guilty, namely, the pretentious disregard for epistemological limits. [APE, 99J, p. 305]

In 1955, Neumann turned fifty and Jung turned eighty. On 23 July 1955, Neumann wrote on the occasion of Jung's eightieth birthday:

A Dutch newspaper that wants to run an article about me has asked me "where I deviate from you, or am of a different opinion." As ever—and I was able to reply in this vein with great delight, I do not see any "deviations" anywhere. Even where I am taking things forward, I am standing, it seems to me, completely on your territory. And I must say, isolated as my position is, both externally and internally, I constantly consider this interweaving with your work as one of the finest gifts of my life. And I know that even where you see accents differently from the way I do that I am someone who, in your eyes, is taking it forward. I have now got used to being this and enjoy being it and I hope this is also true for you. Now this is the only thing that I can give you for your birthday . . . [APE, 104N, p. 313]

In the same year Emma Jung died. On 10 December 55, Neumann wrote a letter of condolence to Jung. He tells him of the special relationship between him and Emma Jung:

Although I only got to know your wife in the last years, from 1948, I think, for me Zurich has been curiously changed without her. She was the conscience, something one could rely on in gloomy Zurich, something solid and full of interest and understanding, . . . [APE, 106N, p. 315]

He goes on in a rather sad tone, having told Jung about the death of his mother some days before:

The world is changing and one is getting palpably older. Both our children are now studying in Jerusalem. Everything is different. Perhaps I am getting a hint of how you are more and more forced to rise above everything so that only nature is left. It is good for me to know that at least Aniela J. is in your orbit. It was painful to me as seldom before to be so far away, for my gratitude toward your wife is great. I am happy that your wife died without much suffering, also happy for you yourself. I know this worry. My mother had a malignant stomach tumor, without knowing it, and died above all from heart failure. How much I would like to see you and speak with you! [APE, 106N, p. 315]

Jung's immediate reply on 15 December 1955:

Please accept my deeply felt thanks for your warm letter! Allow me to express to you for my part my sympathy on the loss of your mother. Unfortunately I can only lay barren words before you, as the shock I have experienced is so great that I am unable either to concentrate or to rediscover my ability to express myself. I would like to have told your friendly open heart that two days before the death of my wife I had—what one could call—a great epiphany. [APE, 107J, p. 317]

In October 1956 the Sinai war between Israel and Egypt broke out, and Jung sent a concerned telegram to Neumann to which Neumann responded with an immediate short letter on 12 November 1956:

I would like to send you just a quick greeting, as at the moment peace reigns and we are all well. My son who participated in the

Sinai campaign is studying medicine in Jerusalem again, and the work here is continuing. Your telegram moved and comforted me, a thousand thanks for it, it arrived quickly and reached us at a time when such a sign of solidarity was more necessary and affected us more deeply than at any other time. A letter about the problems that we discussed when I was last with you is slowly taking shape, it needs time.

I hope you are well, even in Switzerland the fear of Russia seems to have increased very much, it hangs above us like a cloud, but this seems to belong to our fate. [APE, 110N, p. 322]

Half a year passed before Neumann next wrote to Jung on 25 May 1957:

It has now been some time since I received and, of course, also read your fine text *Present and Future*. In my opinion you have succeeded in an enviable way in saying the most vital thing in a popular, comprehensible form. Precisely because I know so well how difficult that is, it is important for me to place at the beginning this "technical" thing that is, however, so essential in reality. [APE, 111N, P. 324]

And later he adds:

For me personally it was a pleasure, besides, that your text extends a hand to my *New Ethic*, which fared so badly, even if in secret, of course. For if a reader of your work now asks himself, so what can actually be done, then he comes up against the problems that compelled me to this work back then in the second world war, with Rommel at the door. [APE, 111N, P. 324]

Jung replied to Neumann on 3 June 1957:

In relation to the so-called *New Ethic* we are basically quite in agreement, but I prefer to express this delicate problem in a rather different language. It is not really a question of a "new" ethic. Evil is and always remains the thing one knows one should not do. Man overestimates himself unfortunately in this respect: he thinks it is within his discretion to intend good or evil. He can persuade himself of this, but in reality he is, in view of the greatness of these opposites, simply too small and too unconscious to be able to choose the one or the other in free will and under all circumstances. It is much more the case that he does or does not do the good that he would like to for overwhelming reasons, and that in the same way, evil just happens to him like misfortune.

Ethics is that which makes it impossible for him to do evil intentionally and encourages him to do good—and indeed often with little success. [APE, 112J, p. 327]

Toward the end of his letter he writes:

I am just occupied with a work that has a completely different theme, but the discussion has meant that I had to also mention the ethical problem. I could not do otherwise than embark on a repudiation of the expression "new ethic," without naming names. This is once again one of those sins, a faithlessness as it were, which imposes itself like a disaster at the moment when I had to protect the disproportionately higher aspect of our psychology from the coarseness of vulgar appreciation and, this, to general advantage. The entire difficulty lies in this case in the slipperiness of the language. Therefore one is forced to strew sand, which occasionally also lands in the eyes of the audience. [APE, 112J, p. 329]

Neumann learns from this letter that Jung does not in fact really understand and accept his notion of the new ethic, and he replies with an excited and heated letter that is hardly scientific but rather touches upon the realms of faith.

Neumann to Jung on 14 June 1957:

I am very moved by your quick reply to my letter, and since the problem broached concerns me very much I would like to try to clarify my position somewhat in the debate with you. While I concur in much, I have the feeling that, for me, it is still about something else than it is for you, or that something threatens to obliterate for me what I have to hold on to when compared with your formulation. Let's start with the main event. *The New Ethic* was the attempt to process a series of phantasies that roughly corresponded timewise with the exterminations of the Jews, and in which the problem of evil and justice was being tossed around in me. . . . then I have to live with the single eye of the Godhead and also to experience the darkness of the abyss. But then evil is not a sin, but part of the world to be experienced. That is not "putting a brave face on it," but reverence before the numinosum of the Godhead, in which I am also implicated with the knowledge that there is no justice and no judge because the measure of God's eye surpasses all this. A moral attitude and human dignity no longer consist in "not exciting any bother," hiding something etc., but in enduring the responsibility for action in the certainty that behind it all there is one hidden who is superior to me who guides me, and what is required from man is to follow the instructions in vigilance and in willingness even to be destroyed. To tear down old gods is not a sin, but it is exactly the reverse that is a sin,—not to place oneself at the disposal of the new aspects of the divine. [APE, 113N, pp. 331–332]

And then:

I believe that the old concept of sin has become untrue, it is no longer effective, and that is not due to the decline of man but to his new understanding of himself and of God. Are these not also "new"? The settlement of the debt that I also believe in is simply not a punishment but the expression of a moral in man that compels him to integration in which even evil is included. If you thus express yourself against *The New Ethic*, then please name names and I will reply if it is necessary, in good faith, for I believe that faithlessness exacts revenge, and would not even know why it would be necessary between us. [APE, 113N, pp. 333]

He accuses Jung of being faithless; however, he closes with: "In old faithfulness and friendship."

As one can clearly understand from his reaction, Neumann was hurt, but he accepted Jung's apology about his so-called "faithlessness . . . to general advantage" and forgave him.

In 1958 an international psychology congress took place in Barcelona, and Neumann gave a lecture there. After the congress he wrote on 11 October 1958 to Jung: "But in Zurich I was able to read the

piece of autobiography *written by you*." [APE, 117N, p. 340] He continued with:

> On c. 20th October we will be in Zurich, I have a "Fear" lecture at
> the Institute on 4th Nov. that I must still write. But I would like to
> be able to speak with you twice, if it is at all possible for you, I am
> also writing to Aniela J., and am looking forward to it very much.
> My link with you is, as you know, not dependent on writing and
> speaking, or no longer dependent, I should say, but meeting with
> you always brings me a substantial affirmation that cannot be found
> anywhere else in the world. I hope you understand what I mean.
> Even the Jungian Congress, which was so positive, only confirmed
> this for me. For me, there is only you yourself as a "connecting
> point" in the center, as far as the task of the work is concerned.
> [APE, 117N, pp. 341–342]

Neumann had no ambivalent feelings toward Jung. He was now
fifty-three years old, a self-made, highly respected, independent author and researcher. But he continued to be always very grateful for a
significant affirmation which could not be found anywhere else in the
world.

Neumann wrote his last letter to Jung on 18 February 1959 after he
had read Jung's manuscript *Memories, Dreams, Reflections*:

> For me, it is the finest thing you have written. I must however ad-
> mit that this is for personal reasons because I do not know anything
> else in writing that is closer to me and to the nature of my life ex-
> perience. You will not perceive this as immodesty for it is not here
> a question of differences in dimension, but of the nature of life ex-
> perience, and you know well how closely the "myth" I wrote when
> I was 16 led to all of this, and if I survey my development as I get
> older and trace its stages, I have a very similar experience of life as
> the one that speaks out of this book. [APE, 118N, p. 343]

Despite the identification and admiration, Neumann maintained
the right to think differently, not to agree, and to argue, without fear-
ing that the differences in opinion would spoil the relationship and
distance them from each other.

If I now bring some comments, "objections," etc., you will understand these as questions that cannot be avoided. They must be asked, for the depth of these things that affect me cannot not remain without reaction, and it seems to me that I must direct this question back to you. But none of my questions should place a burden of a reply on you; you know, that in all these things I have nothing to expect from you but everything from myself. Some of it seems to me to be explained by my Jewish and thus more Eastern background that does not quite overlap with your Christian and more Occidental one. [APE, 118N, p. 343]

And later:

From there on, I have issues about your sentence: "On Life after Death," p. 31: Natural history tells us [. . .] Of course, taken as a whole it is indisputable, "haphazard and casual transformation" seems to me, however, to be a Darwinist remnant that I do not believe in without having a counterthesis to hand. This aspect of the 19th century will perhaps be superseded by a completely different theory in which your conception of the archetype as well as absolute and extreme knowledge will play a crucial role. The development theory takes as its starting point the inadequate and only the rational experience of the historical ego and was not capable of explaining the development, not through chance, selection, and mutation. This is why to speak of an "apparently senseless biological turmoil" seems to me to be a metaphysical statement from you that you otherwise avoid. If the purpose of individual life presupposes such an advanced development in the direction of the Self, then it seems to me we may not any longer go beyond this question after the individual purpose. We are not responsible for it as an isolated, unique historical ego, and the mythical statement of the unconscious sounds completely different. Besides this we have, moreover, no satisfactory explanation, but the composition of the natural kingdoms in which the experience of the world is becoming ever more extensive seems to me to speak against the fact that the way toward the manifestation of meaning, thanks to warm-bloodedness and brain development, has been found by accident. . . .

For this reason I am glad to rediscover also in your work the—unavoidable—"new" ethic in "Late Thoughts" p. 2. This problem of evil will not let me off the hook and is forever making a reappearance in my imagination. Most difficult to swallow. "The murderer can have an epiphany by murdering and the murdered by being murdered," and if I am told "It makes no difference to the light of God if it burns on a black or a white candle," then I have almost dropped out of the Western world, almost out of Judaism, and I do not know from where else but not out of myself—or so I hope. The light wishes to illuminate, it creates dark bodies with the possibility that they will radiate light, is that a primordial mess? I believe the horizontal historical view confuses everything here, life itself is, after all, devouring and being devoured. The only thing that remains open to question is why creation, the answer, radiating in infinite variety what only radiates in itself in an unreflected way, is ancient, but satisfies me. [APE, 118N, p. 345–347]

Jung replied to this excited and enthusiastic letter with an expansive response in which science and faith are conflated with each other. Jung to Neumann on 10 March 1959:

Without the reflective consciousness of man, the world is of gigantic meaninglessness because man, in our experience, is the only being who can detect meaning.

. . . .

Since a creation without the reflective consciousness of man has no recognizable meaning, with the hypothesis of the latent sentience a cosmogonic significance is extended to man, a true *raison d'être*. If, on the other hand, the latent meaning is attributed to the creator as a conscious plan of creation, then the question arises: why should the creator contrive this whole world phenomenon as he already knows what he could be reflected in and why should he reflect himself since he is already conscious of himself? To what end should he create a second, inferior consciousness alongside his omniscience? In a sense, billions of dull little mirrors of which he knows in advance what the picture will be like that they will reflect back? [APE, 119J, pp. 349–350]

This was the last letter exchanged between Jung and Neumann and the only one in which Jung addressed Neumann as "Dear Friend."

Erich Neumann died in Tel Aviv on 5 November 1960 after a short illness. He was not yet fifty-six years old. Jung died on 6 June 1961, also after a short illness, at his house in Küsnacht. He was eighty-six years old.

Thus this fascinating story of the relationship between these two personalities comes to an end. In contrast to the very complicated, ambivalent, and painful relationship between Freud and Jung, the relations between Jung and Neumann were much simpler and uncomplicated. Jung respected and supported Neumann. He regarded him as a colleague, as a creative personality equal to himself, as a successor, and as someone who took his work forward, and in no way as a dangerous opponent. He even protected Neumann to some degree from envious and competitive students in Switzerland.

Similar to the way Freud's affection for Jung, his gifted Christian student, caused envy in Freud's Jewish circle in Vienna, Jung's affection for Neumann, the Jew, and his support of him caused envy among Jung's Christian students in Zurich. While he did not abandon his support of Neumann, there were events in which he acted diplomatically, secretly encouraging and supporting Neumann, while publicly distancing himself and expressing reservations.

Neumann respected Jung as an outstanding, creative personality and a man with especially high culture and human values. He felt a long-lasting, sustained sense of gratitude toward him and protected their good relationship as something especially important and valuable.

Jung symbolized for him the only remaining positive attachment with treacherous Europe. Even when he felt abandoned by Jung, which can be seen clearly in his letters, he retained his positive feelings and relationship with Jung.

It is evident how Neumann differentiated between Jung, the good, on the one hand, and the evil Jung Institute on the other. Neumann made great efforts to protect and maintain the positive significance of Jung for his life by means of this distinction. He did not accept the fact of Jung's anti-Semitism, indeed even denied it. But he forgave him for this reason and sought to explain it as a mistake or an error. "Great men make great mistakes," he said. Neumann sensed strong feelings of closeness and similarity on the inner spiritual, emotional level between him and Jung. He could identify with Jung, despite the great differences between them. Neumann never minimized these differences and always emphasized them in his letters very clearly.

The positive father-son relationship developed into a true friendship, with great mutual affection, warmth, and respect. Jung represented for Neumann the culture of the West in its highest form and best significance, even if distanced and alienated from Judaism.

Neumann regarded himself as a European Jew, deeply rooted in Western culture but unwilling to assimilate to it. He believed he had to seek his Jewish roots and find them in the collective national existence of the Jewish people. Neumann saw in Zionism and in the life and building of Israel the true and only answer and solution for the modern, liberal Jew who is seeking his own identity and who refuses to assimilate.

Notes

1. M. Neumann, "Freud and Jung: An Encounter between Two Personalities," *Sichot: Israel Journal of Psychotherapy*, 2(1987): 5–15.

2. C. G. Jung, *Letters, Volume 1: 1906–1950*, edited by Gerhard Adler and Aniela Jaffé, translated by R. F. C. Hull (Princeton, NJ: Princeton University Press, 1992); C. G. Jung, *Letters, Volume 2: 1951–1961*, edited by Gerhard Adler, translated by Jeffrey Hulen (Princeton, NJ: Princeton University Press, 1976); C. G. Jung, *Selected Letters of C. G. Jung, 1909–1961*, selected and edited by Gerhard Adler in collaboration with Aniela Jaffé, translated by R. F. C. Hull (Princeton, NJ: Princeton University Press, 1984); and C. G. Jung and Erich Neumann, *Analytical Psychology in Exile: The Correspondence of C. G. Jung and Erich Neumann*, edited and introduced by Martin Liebscher, translated by Heather McCartney (Princeton, NJ: Princeton University Press, 2015).

3. For more on this painful subject, see M. Neumann, "The Relationship between Erich Neumann and C. G. Jung and the Question of Anti-Semitism," *Analytical Psychology*, 2(1992): 3–23.

4. C. G. Jung, "The State of Psychotherapy Today" (1934), in *The Collected Works of C. G. Jung*, volume 10, *Civilization in Transition* (Princeton, NJ: Princeton University Press, 1964).

5. The typescript for this letter has the date of 23 April 1935 handwritten at the top of the page, but it is unclear whether it was added by Neumann or someone else.

6. Jung, *Letters, Volume 1*, 518.

7. From the Neumann Papers, private collection, Rali Loewenthal-Neumann, Jerusalem; in Jung and Neumann, *Analytical Psychology in Exile*, xlv.

8. C. G. Jung, "Foreword to Neumann: *Depth Psychology and a New Ethic*" (1949), translated by R. F. C. Hull, in *The Collected Works of C. G. Jung*, volume 18, *The Symbolic Life* (Princeton, NJ: Princeton University Press, 1976), pars. 1408–1420.

9. C. G. Jung, "Foreword to Neumann: *The Origins and History of Consciousness*" (1949), translated by R. F. C. Hull, in *The Collected Works of C. G. Jung*, volume 18, *The Symbolic Life* (Princeton, NJ: Princeton University Press, 1976), pars. 1234–1237.

10. S. Freud and C. G. Jung, *The Freud-Jung Letters: The Correspondence between Sigmund Freud and C. G. Jung*, edited by William McGuire; translated by Ralph Manheim and R. F. C. Hull (Princeton, NJ: Princeton University Press, 1974), p. 245 (letter 330J).

Bibliography

All extracts from the correspondence between C. G. Jung and Erich Neumann are taken from *Analytical Psychology in Exile*, except where otherwise noted. Each letter is annotated with the abbreviation "APE," followed by the letter number and page number(s).

Freud, S., and Jung, C. G. *The Freud-Jung Letters: The Correspondence between Sigmund Freud and C. G. Jung*. Edited by William McGuire. Translated by Ralph Manheim and R. F. C. Hull. Abridged by Alan McGlashan. Princeton, NJ: Princeton University Press, 1974.

Jung, C. G. "Foreword to Neumann: *Depth Psychology and a New Ethic*" (1949). Translated by R. F. C. Hull. In *The Collected Works of C. G. Jung*, volume 18, *The Symbolic Life*. Princeton, NJ: Princeton University Press, 1976.

Jung, C. G. "Foreword to Neumann: *The Origins and History of Consciousness*" (1949). Translated by R. F. C. Hull. In *The Collected Works of C. G. Jung*, volume 18, *The Symbolic Life*. Princeton, NJ: Princeton University Press, 1976.

Jung, C. G. *Letters, Volume 1: 1906–1950*. Edited by Gerhard Adler and Aniela Jaffé. Translated by R. F. C. Hull. Princeton, NJ: Princeton University Press, 1992.

Jung, C. G. *Letters, Volume 2: 1951–1961*. Edited by Gerhard Adler. Translated by Jeffrey Hulen. Princeton, NJ: Princeton University Press, 1976.

Jung, C. G. *Selected Letters of C. G. Jung, 1909–1961*. Selected and edited by Gerhard Adler in collaboration with Aniela Jaffé. Translated by R. F. C. Hull. Princeton, NJ: Princeton University Press, 1984.

Jung, C. G. "The State of Psychotherapy Today" (1934). In *The Collected Works of C. G. Jung*, volume 10, *Civilization in Transition*. Princeton, NJ: Princeton University Press, 1964.

Jung, C. G., and Erich Neumann, *Analytical Psychology in Exile: The Correspondence of C. G. Jung and Erich Neumann*. Edited and with an introduction by Martin Liebscher. Princeton, NJ: Princeton University Press, 2015. [APE]

Neumann, M. "Freud and Jung: An Encounter between Two Personalities." *Sichot: Israel Journal of Psychotherapy*, 2(2), 5–15.

Neumann, M. "The Relationship between C. G. Jung and Erich Neumann According to Their Correspondence." *Harvest: International Journal for Jungian Studies*, 52(2): 36–75.

Neumann, M. "The Relationship between Erich Neumann and C. G. Jung and the Question of Anti-Semitism." *Analytical Psychology*, 2(1992): 3–23.

CPSIA information can be obtained
at www.ICGtesting.com
Printed in the USA
BVHW040211030420
576772BV00016B/847